GUIDE

FOR

Catholic Young Women

ESPECIALLY FOR THOSE

WHO EARN THEIR OWN LIVING

BY

THE REV. GEORGE DESHON

Congregation of St. Paul, the Apostle

Thirty-fifth Edition, Revised

1910

PREFACE.

IN the course of my work as a missionary priest, for many years past, I have been brought in contact with many thousands of all classes of the community.

Among them all, none have interested and encouraged me more than the girls who earn their living by their own hard labor.

I have often admired the beautiful examples of Christian virtue and character I have found among them; their heroic patience and contentment with their lot; the innocence and purity of their lives; their noble self-denial and disinterestedness, and the singleness of mind with which they look above this world and aspire to perfect themselves in the love of God.

This has led me to wish to do something for them; to contribute what little I could to lay a solid foundation in some, and to increase in others what has been already well begun, so that they may become beautiful and fragrant flowers in the garden of the Lord.

I feel that my work will not be in vain,

for the hearts of these good girls are a good soil, which, as Scripture says, receives the seed of the Word with thankfulness, and produces abundant fruit.

My work has been a pleasant one, and I have striven to keep but one thing in view, and that is to do as much good as possible.

If the good girls for whom I have written it find pleasure and profit in it, my whole purpose will have been accomplished.

ST. PAUL'S, 59TH STREET.
Feast of St. Teresa, October 15, 1868.

Preface to the Twenty-fifth Edition.

IT is now more than twenty years since this book has been published.

Its reception by the public for whom it was written has been very gratifying. It had a large sale in the beginning, and it still continues, so that more than twenty thousand copies have been sold.

Scarcely any effort has been made to make it known, but I have received many letters of warm approval from those who have read it. One of our most prominent Bishops told me that he had preached it from cover to cover in conferences to his Young Women's Sodality.

It has also been translated and published in German in Europe. These tokens of approval have encouraged me to revise it carefully, to correct some portions, and add others to make it more widely useful. If those who read it find edification and pleasure in the perusal I hope they will not forget to pray for me.

St. Paul's, 59th Street,
April 6, 1892.

CONTENTS.

CHAPTER I.

A GOOD GIRL HAS REASON TO BE SATISFIED WITH HER CONDITION IN LIFE.

"WHY was I not born rich?" says the poor girl who has to work hard for a living. "There are the ladies, with little or nothing to do, amusing themselves all day and enjoying all the good things of life, while poor I must drudge the whole blessed day, from early morning till late at night, for a living, and a scant one at that. I wish the Almighty had placed me in some better condition of life than the one I am in!"

My good girl, you who talk in that way, you do not think what you are saying. Instead of complaining of the good God, if your eyes could only be opened to see things as they really are, your heart would leap for joy and your tongue would praise Him that you have not been made a lady, or anything but just what you are. For the truth is, your condition of life is one of the very best in which God could place you, and it is a great privilege for you to be in it rather than in any other.

This may seem strange, but let us look into it and see how it is. I dare say you remember that among almost the first words of the little catechism the question is asked: ''For what were we created?'' The answer to it is: ''To learn to serve and love God in this world in order that we may be happy for ever with Him in the next.'' Ah, this lets us into the whole secret! We were not created to be rich, to live without work, to live in fine houses, and wear fine clothes, and ride in elegant coaches, and have what folks are apt to call a fine time of it. No; it was for nothing of all this, but to learn to love and serve God during this life, in order to earn heaven and prepare ourselves to be happy for ever with God.

This is the reason why the rich are so often unhappy, in spite of their money and splendor. They are just living for riches and pleasure, instead of to please God, and they cannot find any real satisfaction in such a life. God will never let us have any real happiness unless we live in order to please and love Him.

It is true a rich man or woman can serve God and be happy, but it is difficult, for riches and honors and pleasure steal away the heart, and cause Him to be forgotten. And when God is forgotten what enjoyment can there be of life?

What is over and above our necessary and suitable clothing will bring but little satisfaction. It only feeds an idle vanity, destroys contentment, and fills us with desires for a thousand things that never satisfy us when they are supplied.

We are always the worse for it when we eat or drink much more than is necessary for us; we lose our appetite, our health, and our strength, so that the body becomes a burden and life a misery.

All the money or honor in the world cannot insure health or contentment of mind.

Then there is death, in the midst of our earthly enjoyments, always staring us in the face. Our friends are cut down around us, and we know not the day or the hour when our turn will come. But we know very well that when it does come we must be torn away, whether we will or no, from everything in this world which we have set our hearts upon. Can we have any enjoyment in such a life as we have here, unless it be grounded on peace with God? unless we carry out the blessed intentions which God had in creating us, namely, that we should love and serve Him?

And then think of that vast eternity which stretches away beyond, after this life is over. How small and mean everything here is in comparison with it! What difference will it make to us when we are once in the presence of God, clothed with glory and honor, with white garments, and the palm of victory in our hands, with no sorrows, sighs, or tears to be feared any more for ever—what difference will it make whether we had a little more or a little less on this earth? Why, this whole life will seem a small speck in the grand ocean of eternity.

In short, in considering any state or condition, the principal thing is, to take into account the advantages it holds out for securing a holy and pious life, so that we may come safe through all the trials and temptations of this world to our only true home in heaven.

In this view, I do not know any among the ordinary conditions of life so good and desirable as that of a life of service or of daily labor.

CHAPTER II.

ADVANTAGES OF A LIFE OF LABOR.

A LIFE of labor has always been considered, by spiritual persons, most favorable to the soul. To have nothing which we are obliged to do may seem very fine to our worldliness and love of ease, but it is most dangerous. You know the old saying: "The devil finds work enough for idle hands to do." It is most true. Idleness opens the door for the worst temptations.

Suppose you had pretty much all your time to do what you pleased with, how likely it is that a great part of it would be misused! Habits of idleness would be formed, your time would hang heavy on your hands, and you would not know what to do. You would seek for amusement; you would soon be altogether taken up with it, and your whole life would become one given up to the world and to wickedness. You would, indeed, stand a great chance of going straight down to perdition.

The labor of the hands is, then, a source of blessing. It furnishes a great help to spending life in innocence. It fills up our time with honest industry, while it leaves the soul free to raise itself from time to time to God. The labor of the hands is not like that of the head. Head-work fills the mind, and takes up its attention, but hand-work leaves the mind in a great measure free.

St. Anthony was taught this by an angel from heaven. One day when he felt tired of uninterrupted prayer, and unable to continue it, he grieved over it before the Lord, and begged to be instructed how to get over this trouble, which was a hindrance to his salvation. After his prayer he went out of his cell, and saw a person, the exact image of himself, seated at work making mats out of palm-leaves, and from time to time rising up to pray. The saint perceived it was an angel who took this form and acted in this manner to make him understand how, by going from work to prayer, and from prayer to work, he could cheerfully and surely work out his salvation.

The old hermits of the desert all understood this. They did not dare to be idle, but made baskets, cultivated the ground, spent all their time in labor or prayer, and so worked out their salvation in the utmost security.

We cannot have the life of these old hermits of the desert over again nowadays, but, outside the walls of the convent, whose life is most like theirs? That of the good girl who earns her own living at some honest employment. She it is who enjoys, more than any others that I know of, the advantages which these old saints coveted so much—who can spend her days in work and prayer, and thus keep off the evil one, and work out her salvation with comparative ease.

Do not, then, complain of labor, but rejoice and thank God that He has given you not a life of idleness, but of honest and continual labor. It is a very great favor of His love, as you will see when this body of the flesh falls away, and you stand on the other side of eternity.

CHAPTER III.

"AH ! but you do not consider what it is to be
constantly working; to be looked down
upon as an inferior; to be treated with contempt : all those things that belong to a life of
labor. Surely it is more than one can put up
with ! And remember it is these very things
that make the life of a working-girl different
from every other. What advantage can there
be in all this ? "

I have taken all these things into account, and yet I say that, in the view of religion, in the view of faith, in the view of Jesus
Christ our Saviour, it is that very humility of
your state, that very subjection to those very
insults, and all that you are liable to suffer,
which make the highest privilege of your condition. These very things are precious dia-
monds and pearls, which the Lord gives to you
and not to others. Why, this is the very
money put in your hands with which you can
buy your salvation ! Only take these things
from the hands of God with patience and thankfulness, and nothing more is required of you.

In this view, how much harder is the lot of your employers than yours! They must be humble and poor in spirit; they must put away pride and haughtiness, or they cannot get through the gate of heaven. "He that exalteth himself shall be humbled" (St. Luke xiv. 11). Think how hard this must be, surrounded as they are by all those things that nourish and increase pride.

Suppose you were in their place, do you think you would be humble and lowly before God; gentle and kind to those below you; not taken up and engrossed with riches; in a word, poor in spirit? I am afraid not. It seems to me it would be very difficult, and so it seemed to our Lord when He thought over it, for He exclaimed, "How hard it is for the rich to enter the kingdom of God!" (St. Mark x. 23).

Be thankful, then, instead of repining, and say, "No, Lord, I ask no change; it is better for me just as I am. I am humbled in the sight of men, but blessed in Thine."

There is a beautiful passage of Scripture which in a few words confirms all that I have said: "But God hath chosen the foolish things of the world that He may confound the wise; and the weak things hath God chosen that He may confound the strong; and the mean things and those that are contemptible hath God chosen" (1 Cor. i. 27, 28).

How beautiful! What the world esteems foolish, and weak, and mean, and contemptible, that is just what God has chosen, what He regards with peculiar favor, what He gives his blessing to and makes to be the road to everlasting life.

Moreover, our Lord shows us this by His own example. Instead of coming into the world rich and noble, He came poor and despised. Instead of coming to be waited upon, He came to wait on others. They used to say of Him: " Who is that? Only the son of Joseph, the carpenter!" They remembered always how they had seen Him carry boards, and help Joseph at the carpenter's trade.

St. Paul says we ought to think in this respect as Jesus Christ did: " For let this mind be in you which was also in Christ Jesus; who, being in the form of God, thought it no robbery Himself to be equal to God: but debased Himself, taking the form of a servant " (Phil. ii. 5, 6, 7). Above all other names, you see, he chooses to be called by the name of " servant."

In the Scripture the life of labor is taken under the special protection of the Lord. Whatever you do for an earthly master is considered by Him as being done for Himself. " Whatever ye do, do it from the heart, as to the Lord, and not to men : knowing that ye shall receive of the Lord the reward of inheritance '' (Col. iii. 23, 24).

What a privilege ! what dignity and honor this throws around your state of life ! When I think of it, I cannot help envying the good girl at work all the numerous advantages she enjoys; her opportunity for retirement and prayer; her opportunity for patience and humility, which will make her so much like Jesus Christ and so dear to Him; her opportunity of acquiring such rich merits by fidelity and good intention in her employments; the safety and peacefulness of her life; and all the good she will do to others by the force of her modest and holy example.

How well the saints understood this ! St. Serapion sold himself twice in succession to the lowest comedians, and served them in the meanest offices, until by his humble example he converted them into fervent Christians. St. Alexius, of a noble Roman family, fled away from his father's house, and after remaining many years, until entirely forgotten, returned and lived seventeen years as a beggar dependent on the charity of his own father, who only found out who he was by a writing found upon him after his death. But I have found a most beautiful example, which throws light on the whole matter and which I will relate more at length.

CHAPTER IV.

EXAMPLE OF SAINT ISIDORA.

THIS holy virgin lived in the Convent of Tabenna, in Egypt. She was one of a community of four hundred sisters. Such was her love of humiliation and contempt that she courted every way and opportunity of abasing herself.

But, as her intention was entirely good, she took care that her follies should all be of an innocent character. She wrapped an old rag around her head, went barefoot, and instead of sitting down at the table like the others, she ate the crumbs which she collected with a sponge and the scrapings of the dishes.

All the time she worked at the hardest and lowest work, as if she had been the vilest slave, and no one ever saw her idle a moment.

Some of the sisters treated her harshly whenever they met her, thinking her to be insane, and others avoided her because they thought her possessed of the devil; but the humble Isidora never made the least complaint. On the contrary, the more ill-usage she got, the more she seemed to be pleased and satisfied.

She exercised herself in this way a long

time, in what we may call the wise folly of the cross, until God, who exalts the humble, was pleased to manifest her heroic sanctity to a great servant of His, named Pytirion, who had lived many years in the exercise of constant prayer and good works.

An angel appeared to him in the desert where he lived, and told him not to think too highly of himself on account of his devotion and good works; that if he would go to the monastery of women at Tabenna, he would find there a person much superior to himself. This was a woman who, being an object of ridicule, and treated with contempt, never showed the least impatience, but kept her heart constantly united to God, serving her sisters with a wonderful exactness and sweetness, while he, although he never left the desert, allowed his imagination sometimes to run over the whole world.

This venerable old man then went to the monastery, where he was well known by reputation, and asked the superior to have all her religious called together, as he had a special reason for wishing to see them. His request was granted, and they all came with the exception of the very one we have been speaking about. Pytirion looked at them all attentively, but he did not discover the one he looked for. "Are all here?" said he. "Yes," was the answer, "all of us." "You must be mistaken," said he, "for I do not see the one that God manifested to me."

"Oh!" said they, "there is another, but she is only a poor crazy thing who works in the kitchen." "Bring her here," said Pytirion, "and let me speak with her." But she seemed to have a foresight of what was to happen, and was so loath to come that they had almost to drag her along, saying that it was Pytirion that wished to speak with her.

As soon as she appeared, the saint saw in her the marks of holiness that the angel had pointed out, and, filled with respect, he fell on his knees and begged her blessing, calling her "Amma," a name only applied to the spiritual mothers of the monastery. She, on her part, fell on her knees and humbly begged his blessing, thinking him superior to herself, and her master in goodness.

All the religious were filled with astonishment at such a sight. A venerable old man on his knees before one whom they considered a poor crazy creature; they could not believe their eyes. "Father!" they cried, "what makes you do so? Don't you know she is only a fool?" "You are the fools," said Pytirion. "She is better than you, and better than I. She is a true mother in holiness, and would to God that at the day of judgment I may appear as loaded with merit as she is."

At this answer they saw how much they had been deceived, and were touched to the heart, and confessed humbly all the abuse and harsh treatment they had inflicted upon her. Pytirion prayed for them, had a long conversation with the humble Isidora, and went away.

Finding herself after this the object of great respect and veneration on the part of the good sisters, she began to feel uneasy. She knew that labor and contempt were much better for her soul, and made her dearer to God. She could not endure to be thought much of, so she soon left the place and went off where she was unknown, and where, no doubt, she lived the same kind of life of contempt and humility as before. Nothing more was ever heard of her, but God knows all her life and will make it manifest at the last day.

CHAPTER V.

"BUT, father, how can a poor girl like myself be said to be in a good condition of life? I have never had an opportunity to get much learning. This, you must confess, is a great hardship, and it seems to me to stand in the way of leading a good life and getting to heaven, which you say is the very thing we all live for. What have you got to say to that?"

I say that, on the one hand, true wisdom does not consist in human science or knowledge, or in knowing a great variety of things, and on the other, that the want of such knowledge does not make us ignorant.

If you know a few things, such as the truths contained in the Apostles' Creed, namely, that God has created you to be happy for ever, that Jesus Christ loved you so much as to lay down His life for you, and that the only true happiness is to be found in seeking first of all "the kingdom of God and His justice"; and if this knowledge has sunk deep in your heart, so that

24

it comes first to mind and directs your actions to
God, you are very wise and very learned.

The man who has read a thousand books, if
these simple things have not sunk as deep in his
mind as in yours, is not so wise and learned as
you are.

For example, a learned man hears a sermon,
and understands the meaning of every word
and of all the ideas, so that he can talk about it
to the wonder of every one, but nothing of it all
has any practical effect on him. You, on the
contrary, scarcely get the full meaning of a
single sentence, and all long and hard words
fly over your head, but you notice some saying of our Lord Jesus Christ, perhaps this:
"Learn of Me, for I am meek and humble of
heart, and you shall find rest for your soul."
It makes a deep impression: you often recall it
to mind; it makes you mild and gentle, and
more and more so during your whole life.

You have understood that sermon better and
learned more than that man did. You have got
more in that sentence than whole piles of books
contain.

The fathers of the desert, with only the
Scripture, or, may be, only some sentences of it
that they knew by heart, but which they kept in
mind, and felt deeply and acted out, became so
wise and prudent that learned men took long jour-
neys on purpose to get their advice on most

important affairs.   They spoke with such truth and force that their words penetrated the hearts of thousands who came to listen to them.

Knowledge of worldly things often fills the soul with so many distracting ideas that it is difficult to take in the meaning of divine things. "Knowledge puffeth up, but charity edifieth" (1 Cor. viii. 1).

The good girl, who really desires to love God, will be taught by God Himself how to do it.   She will hear the principles of wisdom taught in the church, and from the lips of others, and God will constantly whisper them to her heart, so that she will become very wise.

So Thomas à Kempis, speaking in the person of our Lord, says: "I am the one who teaches how to despise worldly things; to be tired of that which must pass away; to seek that which is eternal; to be wise in regard to eternal things; to fly from honors; to endure scandals without sin; to make one put all his hope in Me; to desire nothing that does not lead to Me, and to love Me in preference to everything else."

Sublime wisdom!   What is all knowledge of all science compared to this?   God, "who resisteth the proud and giveth grace to the humble," will give you this wisdom if you desire it. Improve what opportunities you have for learning to read and acquiring useful knowledge;

but remember that the want of learning and opportunity will not stand in your way if you are truly desirous to be united to God. He can in abundance make up for all such deficiency, and He will do so, for He is goodness and love itself.

Well, then, on all accounts you see that your condition in life is a most advantageous one. I hope you will consider it so, and never allow yourself to murmur at it. Be full of joy and thankfulness, and determine by a good life to get from it all the advantages that the Saviour of the world has intended it should afford you.

In the following chapters we will consider more particularly how to live this good life and gain these eternal rewards.

CHAPTER VI.

NECESSITY OF A DEEP AND SETTLED PRIN-
CIPLE TO CLING CLOSELY TO GOD.

ALL the advantage, all the good of a life of labor depends on your being faithful. Two girls may be in equally good situations, yet one will be contented and happy and growing better every day, while the other will be always complaining and fretting, making herself and everybody else unhappy and getting more and more wicked. Let us look into it and see the reason of all this difference.

These two girls are acting on very different principles. One looks first at this world in everything. Her mind is taken up with the idea of enjoying all the pleasure she can now. She is all the time studying the ease and comfort of the present moment. As soon as any desire rises up in her heart she allows herself to be completely carried away by it, and God and religion have to stand in the background.

The other is in the habit of looking away from this world, and looking first at God. The question with her is, Is it right? is it good for my soul? and not, How do I like it? She takes a calm and holy pleasure in denying herself what is wrong or not good for her, because she knows that her soul is united more closely to God, her only real good, by so doing.

This is the reason of all the difference in their lives—why one is so happy and good, the other so unhappy and sinful ; and this shows the necessity of having a right principle of conduct, a principle good enough, and broad enough, and strong enough to regulate all the actions of our life.

We cannot do better than lay down some such principle. St. Paul had such a ruling principle. He says: '' I do not live any longer, but it is Christ that lives in me '' (Gal. ii. 20). He had Christ so firmly seated in his mind, he had it so much at heart to please Him, that he was able to say that he lived no longer for himself, but for Christ. Here was his fixed principle : he would no longer live for himself, but for Jesus Christ. No doubt he used to say to himself on all occasions : '' Remember, Paul, you are no longer to live for yourself, but for Christ '' ; and it was by acting on this principle that he arrived at such a high state of perfection.

In the same way, if you want to live a good life, you must take care to have some such principle, which shall have the upper hand in your soul and control your whole conduct.

It is no matter how it is expressed—whether one says, " It is better to lose the whole world than suffer the loss of the soul " ; or, " My only real happiness consists in serving God " ; or, " My meat and drink shall be to do the will of God " ; or, " I will look at God and his will first in all I do " ; or, " All my desire is to please God and save my soul " ; all these things mean really the same thing.

They mean only what our Saviour meant when He said, " What shall it profit a man if he gain the whole world and suffer the loss of his soul," or, " What shall a man give in exchange for his soul " (St. Mark viii. 36).

We need some such thought to sink deep in our minds, so deep that it may never be forgotten or lost sight of. Oh! my good girl, do not rest satisfied until you can repeat some such sentiment with your whole soul.

When St. Ignatius wanted to get St. Francis Xavier to devote himself to God he did it in this way. He saw St. Francis, at that time a worldly young man, who thought little of his soul, quite frequently, and managed at every interview to repeat the words : " What shall it profit a man to gain the whole world if he lose his own soul." By and by they began to have their effect, and St. Francis said to himself: " Indeed, what *will* it profit me to gain all worldly distinction if I am lost?" He saw things in their true light, devoted himself to God heart and soul, and became a great saint.

So, my dear good girl, you must strive to possess and fill your soul with the grand principle of living for God, of wishing and striving to please and love God more and more.

You must, as it were, keep your eyes fixed on this mark, that the sight of it may always afford you strength and courage.

Suppose a beautiful house, on a hill-top, surrounded by pleasant groves and gardens of flowers, could be placed in your sight, with the promise that it should be yours after a term of faithful service. If you found that service getting tiresome, you would go to your window, look at that beautiful house, your courage would rise, and your labor would again become lightsome and easy.

So have in your mind's eye the love of the Saviour, that great treasure which will make you rich for all eternity, have it always ready to look at, and I will warrant that all the troubles of life, and all the mischances that may happen to you, cannot hinder your soul from rejoicing at the glorious prospects before you.

Would that we could always bear this in mind! But the trouble is, and I may say the only trouble is, that it is so often forgotten; either lost sight of altogether or for a long time, or seen only so dimly and indistinctly that it appears like a dream and has little or no effect on the mind.

Yes, it is very true; this glorious prospect can always be kept in view if we will, and yet it is often, very often lost from sight. Now, I do not want you to lose sight of it, if others do. Your whole spiritual life, goodness, and happiness depend upon your not losing sight of it. Therefore, you must, like a prudent person, consider within yourself what means you will take to keep it always in view.

CHAPTER VII.

HOW TO COMMENCE TO GROUND THIS PRIN-CIPLE IN THE HEART.

IN the first place, have you already got the idea of living chiefly for God and His love strongly fixed in your mind? If not, then you must begin by getting it so fixed. One cannot keep a thing unless one first gets it.

"Oh, father! I fear I have not got it. Tell me how it is to be obtained."

I am glad you desire it, for the very desire is already a beginning. I will tell you now how to get well started, and whatever else I shall say throughout the book will be telling you how to go on with it.

Well, I know no better way to get a good start than to consider and think over these things in the mind, with many devout longings and desires after God.

If the beautiful residence that I imagined just now were at a considerable distance from you, you would strain your eyes to see as much of it as you could; you would walk as near to it as possible, and if you had a spy-glass you would look at it through that.

So, in the same way, be thinking in your

mind of the great happiness, the immense importance, of fixing your soul in the love of Jesus. Be saying to yourself many times (it cannot be too many) : '' Oh! had I only the riches of the love of Christ.'' Long for the love of Christ, and let the exclamation burst often from your lips : '' O Jesus! Thy love is what I want : let all other love, and all the things of the world, become irksome and distasteful to me, so that only Thy love may rule my soul.''

A few days of such holy longings and heartfelt wishes would not fail to light up and inflame your soul with an ardent desire to love God. This desire would make everything that tends to increase this love pleasant and agreeable to you, no matter how unpleasant it might be otherwise.

These impressions would be deepened if you would keep yourself quiet, and not allow other thoughts and distractions to occupy and dissipate your mind ; if you would take care for a while to avoid much conversation, and from time to time retire, if you have the opportunity, to make a special business of this thinking, and simple, devout prayer to God.

If you had any important business of this world on your mind, you would be glad to get in your room alone, that you might think it over without disturbance. In the same way, steal away by yourself to reflect upon this most important of all things, quietly and without disturbance.

I can speak from experience as to the effect of such a course. I have seen many very careless and sinful people, living in the midst of distractions and occupations, who, being aroused by the word of God on a mission, or elsewhere, have by a few days of earnest desire and prayer become completely changed. Their eyes have been opened, so that their former sins have become hateful to them and their hearts· on fire with the love of God, so that the pleasures of the world were unable to give them satisfaction. I have seen them persevere after this beginning steadily, year after year, until death has put its seal on the blessed work.

There is an old proverb that "still water runs deep"; so I would advise you to keep your mind perfectly quiet and still and tranquil, for then God, the Holy Ghost, will deepen every good impression. The devil loves excitement, and hurry, and noise, and passionate feeling. Keep clear of these things, then, if you wish to advance in goodness.

Even if you have been a great sinner, do not excite yourself too much. In that case, clear your conscience by a humble and sincere confession, in a calm and quiet way, without fretfulness or disturbance of mind, and afterward there need never be any serious anxiety on the subject.

Well, then, I will suppose the conscience at rest, and that the only uneasiness the soul has is, that it does not love God half as much as it desires to—a blessed uneasiness, which causes no trouble, but fills the mind with joy.

We must strive to keep up this desire all the time—in peace, however, that the words of the Saviour may be fulfilled in us: "Blessed are they that hunger and thirst after justice, for they shall be filled" (St. Matt. v. 6). We must not merely hunger and thirst after justice (which is the same thing as the love of God) for a day or a week, and then allow the soul to get filled with the world and its desires, but manage in such a way that this blessed hunger and thirst may go on all the time increasing; that it may take up the heart, so that no room may be left for anything evil; no relish for anything that does not increase this love, and no joy or happiness except it springs from this holy longing and desire that possesses the soul.

Let us see how we may keep up and increase this holy fire after it is once lighted.

CHAPTER VIII.

HOW TO INCREASE IN THE LOVE OF GOD, OR OF PRAYER IN GENERAL.

THE way to do this is very plain and simple. There is nothing about it you cannot easily understand, nothing you cannot easily do. It will depend chiefly on one thing, whether you *pray, and have regular daily habits of prayer.*

By prayer I do not mean going over the words written in a book. No; there may be prayer without the help of a book as well as with it. Prayer means to converse or talk with God, or, as some say, to raise the soul to God.

But what shall we talk with Him about? I will tell you. Faith teaches us who God is and what He is, what He loves and wishes. It teaches that He knows all and can do all; that He loves us; that His love for us is very great, and that on account of this love He redeemed and purchased us with His own blood. It tells us that He came down from heaven and became one of us, lived here in poverty, and suffered and died on the cross to open the gates of heaven to us.

At the same time we know how miserable and poor we are of ourselves, and what constant

need we have of help from God to get along, in
body and soul.

Do you not see, then, how many things we
have to talk to God about; how much to think
about before God? Now, this thinking of God,
talking with Him, this begging of Him what
you need, this is prayer; and you can easily
see that this does not depend on book-learning.

Indeed, if you are accustomed to use a book
when you pray, I would advise you not to read
over the prayers merely, or to go over a great
many at a time, but to pause from time to time
as you go along, and to think and talk with God
as much as you can out of your heart and soul.

One little prayer with a great deal of heart in
it, a great deal of the simple talking of the heart
with God, is worth more than whole pages of
prayers read off without heart from a book.

Now let me give you an example of this. An
old woman came to St. Teresa one day, who
seemed to have something on her mind that
made her feel very bad. "What is the matter?" said the saint. "O dear!" replied the
old woman, "I should like to pray, but I cannot. I can't even get through the Lord's
Prayer. I begin 'Our Father who art in heav-
en'—then I think, *my Father* in heaven! Who
is it that allows me to call Him *Father?* The
great and wonderful God! I think a long
while in astonishment on this. I think what

this name of father means; what love it shows on his part; what a happiness it is to have such a father. I get running on so in my heart that it seems to me I never come to an end, and cannot, for the life of me, finish the prayer.' "

St. Teresa was full of admiration at the old woman's account of her prayer, and told her to go on praying just that very way, for it was• all right, and a great favor from God to be able to pray in that manner.

The fact is, prayer is a very simple thing and suited to all sorts and conditions of men—to the ignorant as well as to those that have learning; to those who cannot read as well as to those who can; to children as well as to grown people. Indeed, the more simple, childlike, unaffected dispositions you bring before God, the easier and better will be your prayer.

So, I do not doubt that there are some good girls, with little learning of books, who, from their great wish to love God, pray easier, love prayer more, and practise it with more constancy and pleasure than many of those who have much learning and a great variety of books to help them.

The hermits of the desert were the great models of prayer. They learned the great secret of praying all the time. And who were they? Mostly very unlearned and simple people, who, while they labored with their hands, in their own simple way talked in their hearts with their God and Saviour.

You see, then, you can pray, no matter what your condition may be. But in order to pray well you must pray regularly and constantly. If you have not a habit of praying, the chance is you will not pray much. It will slip little by little out of your mind, until you drop it entirely.

CHAPTER IX.

DAILY EXERCISES OF PRAYER.—MORNING PRAYER.

BUT you ask me, At what time should I pray? I answer, Begin in the morning when you first get up. Then you are beginning a new day. A great number of things will take place during that day. It may turn out very much to your soul's advantage, or it may be quite the other way. Then it is well early in the morning to make a good start for the day. If a good thought, a holy resolution, or a pious wish gets entrance first into your soul, it will go far to keep everything right during the day, and make it a fruitful one for the love of God and virtue.

Then, as soon as you can after waking, try to think some pious thought or make some pious wish. For example: "God keep me from sin this day," or "May I pass this day so that I shall be more secure of heaven at night!"

When you wash your face and hands, say "Wash me more and more from my sins." When you dress, say "Clothe me with justice, with true virtues, that I may be pleasing in Thy sight." Such practices are very good; they have a greater effect than they seem to have at the time, and prepare the soul for prayer.

When you are dressed, try to get a little time to kneel down and make a prayer to God, to recommend yourself to Him, to beg His protection for the day, to make a good intention to please God in all you do or have to suffer.

"Oh! but I have no time for this. My work is so hard and so pressing. The breakfast must be got so early; I must get off to my work in a hurry." Well, I know this will often be the case—a poor girl will hardly have time, as they say, to turn around; but for all that, take a little time to pray. God will accept a little under such circumstances, and give as much grace as if you had spent more time, for he sees that you have trouble to give Him even that little.

Get up five minutes earlier and give Him that five minutes, and you cannot tell what a benefit it will draw down upon your soul. If you had a dear friend who was going away early in the morning, how gladly you would leave your bed half an hour earlier to bid him good-by. Why not, then, devote at least a few minutes of your sleeping time, if necessary, in order that you may talk with the Blessed Saviour, and get your heart bent and inclined to spend the whole day cheerfully and joyfully in His service.

CHAPTER X.

CONTINUATION.

BUT sometimes one gets up, as they say, wrong foot foremost—that is, one feels so out of sorts, so cross and ill-natured, that one hardly knows what to do with one's self. At such times everything looks dark, and is likely to go wrong ; and many a poor girl who has not the habit of turning to God in prayer is turned all that day to evil, to passion, to dark and melancholy and wicked thoughts. Many a one has lost a good place by simply giving way to such feelings.

It is on such occasions, and they will happen to every one sometimes, that we see the power and loveliness of the habit of offering one's self with fervor to God in the morning. As soon as this dark and melancholy humor comes over one, this offering changes it all into a sweet and calm resignation to the holy will of God.

The dreariness of the world inspires a longing for God and heaven, and all that would foster sin and evil habits of passion now only draws and unites one more closely to God, according to Holy Scripture: "All things work together for good to those who love the Lord" (Rom. viii. 28).

Then never mind how you feel in the morning; if you are out of sorts, if you feel ill-humored and cross, if you feel even wicked and inclined to evil, if praying is burdensome to you—go right on, all the same; cast yourself on God your Saviour; tell Him that at least you desire to be good; that you will not give way to these evil feelings, that you cannot help them; but you wish to be always mild, and good, and gentle, and ask the grace that you may go on and do your duty, and imitate your Lord the same as if you felt ever so devout.

I cannot tell you how much you gain by such a course. These are the very times when we triumph over the devil, when we are dearest to God, advance the most in virtue, and go farthest in fixing the soul, so that it cannot be moved, in all that is good. Then, on no account, though your occupation may give you little time, omit this offering of yourself to God in the morning, and unite yourself to Him with fervor and with your whole soul.

All this is not so easy at first because you are

not accustomed to it, but it will soon become
easy, and you will get so used to it and so fond
of it that you would as soon lose your breakfast
as to omit it. If called away suddenly from
your prayers, your heart would continue to
speak to God, though your hands and feet were
occupied with something else, and you would
perhaps pray with more fervor than if you had
plenty of time at your own disposal.

CHAPTER XI.

RENEWAL OF GOOD INTENTION.

WELL, now, suppose the day begun in this
way, and that with a cheerful and, so to
speak, sweetened heart you go about your daily
labor or occupation. Many a long hour stretches
out before you, and many a distracting thing
will happen before the day closes. What shall
we do in order not to forget or lose sight of those
pious morning resolutions?

The holy Apostle St. Paul tells us we must
"pray without ceasing." And if we could carry
out his precept we should surely be in no danger, since the Lord has promised, and His
promise will surely be fulfilled: "Ask and ye
shall receive," "Call on me and I will help you."

But who can pray without ceasing when
work must go on? When that work takes up

one's time and attention completely, when one can hardly think of anything else, sometimes, for a good while together? That certainly seems asking too much, and more than we can do. Now I do not ask any more than you can do, nor any more than I know you will be glad to do, if you have made a good prayer in the morning.

I said that one should make a good intention in the morning to please God by all one's actions or sufferings during the day. That is beautifully expressed in some such words as these: "O my God! I offer to Thee all the thoughts, words, actions, and sufferings of this day, in union with those of Jesus Christ, with the intention of doing everything only to please Thee."

You see how beforehand, by a pious intention and desire of the heart, you have offered all that may happen during the day to the Lord, and joined all your actions to those of Jesus Christ ; that is, you desire to behave in all things just as Jesus Christ would wish you to behave, or, what is the same thing, to please Him and His heavenly Father.

Now, that good desire is accepted by God and laid to your credit. And although afterwards you may do many things without actually thinking of God, such as eating, drinking, cooking, sewing, standing beside the noisy machine, scrubbing, taking care of children, or any other duty, yet that morning's good intention spreads over them, covers them all with the virtue of holy prayer, and makes them good in His sight.

We "pray without ceasing" through these good intentions. Our sleep is a prayer, if we make an intention to rest ourselves for God's glory, that we may be in better health and strength to serve Him and do our duty. So our eating and drinking, by the same kind of intention, is sanctified and made holy in the sight of God.

Then, always make that good intention in the morning, and renew it from time to time during the day ; saying, " Let all my actions be to please my God," or something else like it. This will soon become natural to you, for having set out to talk with God, He will want to talk with you.

God, the Holy Ghost, will in His still and quiet way put many a good thought and many a good desire in your heart, many a holy sigh and devout prayer on your tongue. All you will have to do will be to listen to that still voice, which will continually be saying to you, " Do this, it is pleasing to God " ; " Let that alone, it will hurt your soul " ; " Pray now a little, that you may keep your soul fixed on your God," and many other such things.

These short prayers, which the Holy Ghost will put in your mind from time to time, will keep your soul awake to God and attentive to please Him, so that you may with truth be said to pray without ceasing, even if for some time you are not conscious of making an actual prayer.

Especially in any time of temptation, when sin of any sort seems pleasant or good to you, will the voice of the Holy Ghost be heard in your soul. " Child of God, beware ! that is a sinful thing ; pray, oh, pray ! for grace to avoid it." Make a habit of attending to that voice within you, of shutting your eyes and ears and your whole mind to that evil temptation. Raise your soul quickly to God, and cry out, " Lord Jesus, help me ! let me not fall into this or any sin !" or simply repeat with devout mind the holy names, Jesus ! Mary !

That cry will quickly reach heaven, and God will send His help and put the temptation to flight.

It is exceedingly important to get in the habit of praying short and fervent prayers at such times. By them we get a great victory over the enemies of the soul, and great strength to persevere, instead of being taken captive and led away in chains, to suffer all that the wicked enemy chooses to put upon us.

CHAPTER XII.

OF PRAYER DURING THE DAY.

BESIDES the times of temptation, if at other times you feel devout, and God stirs up in your heart a desire to pray, you need not feel afraid to give way to it. If you could think of God the greater part of your time, there is no harm, but the greatest blessing and the greatest joy in so doing.

If you can think a good thought, or wish a good wish, in the midst of your cooking or working or house-cleaning or factory-work, be thankful to God for the favor, and make the most of it. It is certainly far better to remember God and eternal things than to be whirled about with a continual excitement in regard to matters of no consequence, and to be forgetful of Him, as some are, from morning till night, from day to day, from week to week, until they almost forget they are Christians.

No: do you go on a different principle; deepen and strengthen good thoughts on all occasions. Let the life of our Lord Jesus Christ here on earth be ever before you. Love to dwell on the particulars of His actions, as they are written down in the Scriptures.

If your work comes hard, remember how He carried a heavy cross all the way up Mount Calvary. If any one speaks evil of you, see Him hanging on His cross, and the rabble underneath calling Him every vile name they could think of. If tired and weary, think how He, after a long, weary travel, had no place where He could lay His head.

Go over His blessed, humble, charitable conversations and discourses, that you may always be learning something new, for your own increase in goodness and in the love of God.

Sometimes it may nourish your soul to think of our Blessed Lady. Imagine her as she goes about the house, always ready to do everything that duty requires of her, always so quiet and peaceable, always taking such delight in doing everything that could please her Maker, and in doing it in the most perfect manner; always so sweet and obliging to all her fellow-creatures. She is, indeed, in a special way an example to you, for it was in doing very much the same things that are required of you that she made herself so dear to God.

Be sure to take advantage of all the usual opportunities of calling God to mind. For example, do not sit down to eat without blessing the food, and do not rise up without giving thanks for it. Our meals in this way become a sort of station or stopping place, to recall to our minds

what we are striving never to forget or lose
sight of. They are very proper and suitable
stations, too, since we should get ourselves in
the habit of thanking God for all His mercies,
and all the means of sustaining this life, which
is given for gaining eternal life hereafter.

CHAPTER XIII.

OF NIGHT PRAYERS.

NOW let us suppose the day has gone by;
that you have done your work; that
everything has been put in order, and that you
have some time to yourself. If the day has
been spent in the way I have been endeavoring
to point out, in remembering God and convers-
ing with Him from time to time amidst your
work, I am sure there is a fire of love burning
in your heart. You have been so busy that you
could not let it blaze up; it has been smoulder-
ing like live coals covered up with ashes, but all
ready to burst out in a bright and warm blaze.

Now, then, is the good time to rake off those
ashes, to put on some fresh fuel and let the fire
burn brightly. Yes! nothing interferes with
the free attention of the soul to God; all the
world is hushed and the darkness of night only
seems to make God nearer to us. We feel our

own helplessness; what mere nothings we are, and God seems all and everything. We understand then more clearly how great, how wonderful, how wise, and how good He is. This is indeed a golden time to raise the soul to God.

Brother Gerard, a lay brother of the Congregation of the Most Holy Redeemer, used to spend whole nights looking up at the stars so bright and wonderful, his heart perfectly filled with love and admiration for God their Creator. Of course you cannot do the like, but the solemn silence of the night invites you to set apart some time, and a more considerable time than at any other part of the day, to devote it to God and your soul.

Then you can cast a look back at the day that has passed, to see how you have spent it; to see what has been wrong, that you may be sorry for it and sincerely resolve to amend it. Recall to mind what good you have done, that you may humbly thank God for it; for it is indeed a source of joy if we have done well, though we must remember that all good comes from the Holy Ghost, and that without Him we could not so much as think a good thought.

This is a time, too, to thank God for all His mercies and for all you have had to suffer, since that is a mercy, if you did but know it; to recommend yourself to His protection for the night, and to give yourself body and soul to Him; to offer Him your life, and your death, at whatever time and in whatever manner may be most pleasing to Him.

Now, there is one caution I must give you, in order that all my advice about your night prayers may not turn out useless. It is a plain thing, but most important. You should have a regular hour for retiring and preparing yourself for your night's rest, and that hour ought not to be a late one. Late hours are the destruction of piety. Fix your hour, and when it comes around retire, that you may commune with God.

Do not run out visiting every evening. If you go out now and then to see your friends and acquaintances, be sure to finish your visit in good time, and get home again at your regular hour for retiring. In the same way, if visitors come to see you, do not let them stay too late. Remind them kindly that it is getting late, and that you are obliged to retire. Bid them good-night, and let them go home, so that they may get to understand that it is no use to come to see you at an unreasonable time.

This is very important, for how can a poor girl talk and talk all the evening until a late hour, without every good impression being driven out of her soul? After such an evening, when she kneels down to pray she will find herself quite distracted; not a good thought will be likely to come into her mind. All the affairs of

Mary, or John and William, or Mrs. This or Mrs. That, a heap of idle, nonsensical thoughts, will be chasing one another in her poor distracted head.

It may be sinful temptations will get such a firm hold on her imagination that the devil will be sure to bring her into some sin, while much of that holy peacefulness that reigned in her soul before is lost.

Shun, then, late hours, shun idle gossiping, slanderous and sinful talk ; and keep your soul in such a state that when the blessed hour arrives to pray, you may find yourself ready, and in a fit mood to enjoy the conversation of God your Saviour.

CHAPTER XIV.

OBJECTIONS ANSWERED.

"OH!" you say, "it would be very well if we could spend our day in pious thoughts and prayer as you have laid it out for us; but if you were obliged, as we are, to work in the kitchen, or in the noisy mill, or to stand at the counter all day, you would soon see that it is much easier to give these directions than to carry them out. You would see that it is a hard thing to recollect one's self at all."

I can well imagine a good-hearted, well-dis-

posed girl, whose temper is lively and some-
what impatient, and who wants to do everything at once, saying something of this kind,
at least in her mind. Now, I say to her, You
are mistaken. Work, and hard work too, will
not interfere with the daily life I have laid
down for you. I do not mean to say that you
can learn to follow it out perfectly all at once,
so that nothing will be left to improve upon.
Nothing is done just in that way.

It took you many years to grow to your full
height. First you were a little baby, and could
not help yourself. Then you had to toddle
about and to walk. Afterwards you were a
little girl without much wit in your head, and
could not work or maintain yourself, but you
kept on growing little by little; you kept on
eating your food and growing, though nobody
could see you grow, until little by little you
came to be what you are now, with the full use
of body and mind.

These holy practices of prayer will be imper-
fect, perhaps, in the beginning, but they will
grow. You may not see how they grow from
day to day, it is such a gradual thing ; but after
some time you can look back and see very
plainly that you have made progress, and that
spiritual things have taken root in your soul,
and the tree of your salvation is growing strong
and healthy. Let me give you an example to

show you that much work, and hard work, cannot prevent your raising your soul constantly to God.

St. Catherine of Siena, when very young, just verging upon the age of womanhood, was very pious, prayed a great deal, and occupied her thoughts with God and heavenly things. She had such a clear insight into the vanity of all earthly things that she determined to live only for Jesus Christ, and never to marry. This did not please her mother and the rest of the family. Her eldest married sister had died suddenly, and they were anxious that Catherine should accept a very advantageous offer, and so take her sister's place in the family.

But she would not listen to such a proposal, and to show how fixed her resolution was she cut off her hair, which was very beautiful. The whole family felt highly displeased. They considered her much too pious. They knew they could do nothing while she prayed so much, so what did they hit upon? They concluded to load her down with work. They sent away the servant, and made her do all the work of the house.

Another person was placed in her room, so that she should never be alone at any time, and they always contrived to send for her, and break up her prayers, when she was seen to commence them. Do you think they succeeded

in cooling her love for God, or lessening her
prayer? Not at all. She went on quietly as
before, did all her work, and prayed at the
same time, in that simple, short way I have recommended, and made more progress in the
love of God than ever before. She did not allow herself to be disturbed, for she built a little
room for herself in her own heart, to which she
retired very frequently, and there she always
found the Holy Ghost waiting for her, and helping her to pray.

They drove her out of her room, it is true,
but they could not drive her out of her own
heart, where God has His dwelling; as the
Scripture says: "The kingdom of God is within you" (St. Luke xvii. 21). And again:
"All the glory of the king's daughter is within" (Ps. xliv. 14).

That is true; all the work in the world cannot hinder you from admiring, loving, and seeking God; cannot hinder you from begging God
for His grace and love. It cannot hinder you
from being daughters of the heavenly King, if
your beauty is within, in the soul; if you make
yourselves beautiful in His sight, by keeping
your hearts directed to Him in the midst of your
occupations, while you are ready to give more
time and attention to prayer, as soon as your
leisure permits you to do so.

CHAPTER XV.

ADVANTAGE OF SPENDING SUNDAY WELL.

WE have seen how to spend the day, united to God by devout sighs and aspirations and holy prayers, amidst all the employments of busy life.

Every week, by God's appointment, there comes around a day especially devoted to His service, and the refreshment of our souls—the Sunday—when labor ceases, in great measure, to give place to devotion and innocent recreation.

What a blessing this is from God! We may compare it to the oasis in the desert. The weary traveller, in eastern countries, sometimes has to make his way through vast regions of barren, heated sand, with no springs of refreshing water, no trees to shade him from the sun, no cool breezes, often for many days, until he is ready to sink down from fatigue and exhaustion; his tongue parched with thirst; his blood on fire with the heat.

In these regions, scattered here and there, are beautiful spots, where clear, fresh water springs from the ground; where delightful fruits, oranges, lemons, dates, grow in great abundance, and the air is cooled by the water springs.

How these travellers long to find these spots! When the camels and other beasts of burden snuff the air from a distance, they forget their fatigue, they run with eagerness to quench their thirst at the cool fountains, and to enjoy the fresh grass. Their owners, with no less delight, stop a day, or several of them, to recruit their strength and cheer up their spirits, that they may be enabled to continue their way until they reach another of these refreshing places. So, they hope, finally, to get through the wearisomeness of the whole journey, and successfully gain all they had in view in setting out.

Our Sundays are to us such cool, delightful spots in the journey of life. The soul is weary of the dust and heat of the world. The soul is fatigued with having so many things to do, and longs for opportunity to rest in God; to satisfy the thirst it has for God. It longs for the cool fountain and the refreshing waters.

Where are they? In the house of God, in the very place where He dwells. There is the altar of God in the church, His house: the burning lights are around it, flowers decorate it, devout worshippers surround it, and all invites the soul to pray.

But what are all the lights and flowers compared to Him who is present in their midst?

The Lord of Glory, the Blessed Saviour Himself, is there.   He has come down on that altar to offer Himself for us ; to pray to His heavenly Father by His wounds and blood most effectually for us, and to remain in the midst of us to hear our prayers and talk with us face to face.

Thus, the Sunday is the time, and the church is the place, for the soul's weekly rest. The good girl, who longs for God's love, will not pass it by.   God in His mercy has commanded that we should take advantage of it. " Remember the Sabbath day to keep it holy." The church, of which the Lord said, " He that heareth you heareth me " (St. Luke x. 16), which is in Christ's place, now that Christ has ascended into heaven, has changed this time of rest from the seventh to the first day of the week, in honor of the Lord's rising from the dead on that day.

The Sabbath of the Jews has given place to the Christian Sunday, but the obligation of keeping one day in the week holy remains the same.   We are bound, then, by the law of God to do so.   But in what way are Christians required to keep the day holy, in order that they may not sin against this law ?   This question I will answer in the next chapter.

CHAPTER XVI.

OF WORKING ON SUNDAY.

WE are required to abstain from servile or hard labor, that is to say, from labor of the hands, and to assist at least once at the Holy Mass on the Sunday. But we must understand what is meant by being forbidden to work on that day. Necessary work, such as belongs to the good order of the house—cooking, making beds, sweeping, and putting things in order—is not forbidden.

The care of the sick is a necessary and charitable work. Sometimes, unless work is done, valuable property would go to destruction. In all these cases work must be done ; and it would be displeasing to God should you refuse to do it on the plea that it is wrong to work on the Sunday.

Indeed, as a general rule, for those who live out, the mistress of the house is a proper judge of what is necessary and what not. She knows many reasons that you do not know, and it is not proper to make her give an account of everything to those in her employment. That would be upsetting the order of things that the Lord has established when He says : " Servants, be obedient unto your masters according to the flesh '' (Eph. vi. 5).

So, if anything of no very great importance comes up, do it cheerfully ; and, depend upon it, the responsibility will not be on your shoulders. On the contrary, the Lord will look on your mild and peaceable disposition, free from all strife and contention, so much like His own, and reward it with special graces.

It is quite another thing when you put off your own work until Sunday. This depends on your own will ; and therefore you, and not any one else, will have to answer for it. To devote Sunday to making up articles of dress, or to a general mending of clothes, is very wrong.

And even if you live in the country, where you cannot attend Mass, the case is not altered ; for the command, '' Six days shalt thou labor and do all thy work,'' applies as well to such cases as to any others. The day everywhere is intended to be devoted to the service of God, and not to work.

But suppose your employer has no sense of what is proper ; makes no distinction between Sunday and another day ; loads you down with work that, it is clear, could as well be done another day : what is to be done in that case ?

Keep quiet, do not fly into a rage, but quietly look around for another place. It may be that, if you spoke about it quietly and without passion, it would be set right ; but if not, look out for another place, where the Lord's day is respected, and when you have found one, give notice peaceably and quietly of your intention to leave.

Perhaps the employer may ask the reason. Do not let your feelings get the upper hand, but tell them with the utmost calmness that your religion requires you to avoid unnecessary work on the Sunday ; that you find so little regard paid to God's commandment in regard to this, that you cannot remain longer. Who knows but that such a mild and firm answer may produce a happy change, and take away the difficulty ? If so, the next girl who comes into their service will not be troubled in the same way.

I need say no more about labor on Sundays, for your own good sense and, more than all, the light of the Holy Ghost, which is given to all who sincerely ask it, must direct you as to the rest.

CHAPTER XVII.

ON ATTENDANCE AT MASS.—EXCUSES FOR NEGLECTING IT.

WHY has the Almighty required His people to abstain from labor on Sunday? Surely it was not in order that they might be quite idle and listless. No! It was in order to afford us a better chance to worship Him and to attend to their souls. Therefore, along with the abstinence from labor is the command to attend to God's service, by hearing at least once the Holy Mass on that day.

How a well-principled girl can neglect this duty is more than I can conceive. How can she be determined to worship God in spirit and in truth, and yet neglect the very highest and best act of worship it is possible to pay?

This is just what the Holy Mass is, in which our Lord Jesus Christ Himself, true God and true man, comes down from heaven upon our altar to offer Himself in sacrifice for our sins, and to give Himself to us in Communion; to renew the very action which He performed when He died for us upon the cross. We are properly required, then, to assist at this most important action, and not let the day go by without having discharged this duty.

You must do so according to the very best of your ability. I say according to the best of your ability, because I know that every one cannot go to Mass every Sunday. Still, I am told by a very truthful and judicious girl, who has had a good deal of experience herself, and is largely acquainted with the circumstances of others, that it is rarely the case, at least in cities and towns, that a good girl who desires it cannot go to Mass every Sunday.

I believe she spoke the truth, and that where there is a will there is a way, and that with a little good management at least one Mass can be heard on each Sunday. In our large cities and towns there are often so many Masses at different hours of the morning that one could select the most convenient, and attend it without neglecting any duty at home.

It may be necessary to rise early, it is true; for there are some girls who cannot well attend any Mass unless they get to the first one. Well, then, get up with cheerfulness and attend to your duty; you will have time enough to rest another part of the day.

I have not much patience with the sleepy-heads, who sleep away their precious time, when duty calls them to be awake. I am sure they cannot have much patience with themselves. They must feel out of sorts and miserable to think they have had so little courage, and so little conscience, as to lie in their beds when they know perfectly well they ought to be up, and that God's voice is calling them away to the church.

My dear good girl, no matter how comfortable the bed may be, no matter how little inclination you may feel to go out, rise at once; seize the opportunity to hear Mass. Be found among the devout worshippers kneeling before the altar, and the good God will not forget it.

The habit of obeying the voice of God in this respect will help you in other respects, and on other occasions. You will be laying solidly the foundations of that mansion which shall be yours eternally in the heavens.

Sometimes your going to Mass will depend on your asking permission, or giving notice in order that matters may be arranged so as to allow you to go. Many a girl keeps silent and loses Mass. Now, that is not right. It is your duty to speak.

It is well to have an understanding on the subject when you enter service at a place, that everybody may be satisfied afterwards. Inquire modestly what can be allowed in this respect, and, depend upon it, your employers will think all the more of you for it.

It happened once that, after a Mission, one

of the missionaries had occasion to call on a Protestant acquaintance. In the course of the conversation the priest remarked: "I fear the constant attendance of your domestics at the Mission has put your wife to some inconvenience." "Yes, it has caused some inconvenience," was the reply, "but we are glad to suffer it, for we know well that the best girls are those who attend to their religious duties the best. We feel it to be right to offer to others the privileges which we prize so much for ourselves."

Every right-minded employer will have such sentiments, and they are held far more commonly than we give them credit for. I do not like to hear of a Catholic girl going off to Mass secretly and slily, as if she were doing something to be ashamed of. No! let her say openly when she is going, and I am confident that in most cases there will be every disposition to arrange things according to her wishes.

Sometimes, where there are a number of girls in the same family, they could all attend Mass, if a spirit of charity prevailed among them, and a disposition to accommodate one another. Why should they not change places sometimes, and one do the other's work while she goes to Mass? How much better is this than that cross and snappish spirit which makes one flare up with pride and anger, and say, "No, I will not!" "You attend to your own work, and I will to mine." "I won't wash dishes for anybody." "I won't have anything to do with taking care of the child. I don't want to be troubled with the cross thing." "I'm going to Mass. What do I care whether you go or not?" "I'm not obliged to be looking out for you." How hateful such things are in the sight of God, who came down from heaven to do good to us all, who has enjoined on us so often to love one another, and to be solicitous for one another's happiness! Is this "bearing one another's burdens," that so we "may fulfil the law of Christ?" (Gal. v. 2). I think not, and I fear that she who attends to her religious duties with such a spirit will get very little profit from them.

The truth is, some girls are glad enough of an excuse to keep away from Mass. They pretend their duties keep them back, and they could go, after all, well enough if they chose to make arrangements to do so.

And here let me caution you as to another fault. A girl is in a good place, where she can and does go to Mass every Sunday, but now and then something occurs to prevent it. She straightway flies into a passion, and declares her intention to quit her place. I know such an instance.

A girl had been living some time in a place

where she was treated with every indulgence, and allowed to go to Mass every Sunday. She had not been required to remain at home a single time until the lady of the house, who was very sick and near to death, required her help one Sunday, after the others had been exhausted in watching. Immediately she refused with great anger; declaring she would not lose Mass for anybody or anything, and that she would not continue to live in the place any longer.

There was no obligation to hear Mass under such circumstances, as she ought to have known, and such conduct was scandalous, giving a very false and hateful aspect to our holy faith, which we all know enjoins the utmost charity to the sick and suffering. That girl's own conscience told her this, for she came the next day acknowledging her fault and asking forgiveness.

When pride and ill-temper put on the cloak of piety and duty, they are more hateful than in their own dress, for then they bring dishonor upon religion and God.

CHAPTER XVIII.

EXCUSES FOR NOT ATTENDING MASS.

I WILL tell you another reason why many do not go to Mass regularly, as they ought. They have no seat in the church, and of course they do not feel at home there. If they had a place to go to, they would not feel ashamed, as they do now, to be seen kneeling in the aisles, or be afraid of being turned out because they are taking up a seat that another has paid for, and which they fear they must give up as soon as he makes his appearance.

It is true there is no class of Catholics better, on the whole, in this respect, than girls who work. They generally do have a home in the church, and it is a real pleasure to see them there, with so much devotion, and evidently so delighted to be near our Blessed Lord and His Holy Mother.

But some, and perhaps a good many, have no seat, and it is for this reason that they often, and very often too, neglect their duty. Now and then conscience speaks loudly to them, and forces them to go to Mass. And then what will you see? A young woman kneeling in the aisle, dressed perhaps in a lilac silk, with a pink

satin bonnet, and an ostrich feather sticking out
at the top of it. What a sight! She is so poor
she cannot afford to pay a small sum for a seat
in the house of God, and why not? Every cent
she can get is laid out in finery to put on her
back, and, to tell the truth, she would look
much better without it.

This reminds me of an excuse that is often
made: "I do not attend Mass, for my clothes
are not suitable." I imagine very few girls,
who have work, will be inclined to say any such
thing, and if they do, I hardly think they can
be saying the strict truth.

Decent clothes may be necessary, but not
fine ones. The church is the last place to go
to, to show off. Many say their clothes are not
good enough, when what they have on is quite
as good as pious and virtuous ladies are content
to wear.

Others say: "I did not go to Mass because I
had no shoes to wear." And why not? Because they have neglected to provide them. So
they go week after week, neglecting their duty
out of sheer laziness and inattention.

If tempted to vanity on the score of clothing,
remember the Blessed Virgin. The thought of
her will put all such proud and foolish notions
out of your head.

Another says she has missed Mass because
something happened, just as she was getting

ready to go, that put her out of temper, and she
felt so confused and "all of a tremble" that
she just stayed at home. "What use would it
be to go in such a state of mind?" she says.
All the use in the world. What! because
one sin is committed, shall we give ourselves
headlong to commit many others? That is indeed a poor way to get along. No such reason
excuses you from your obligation.

The right thing for you to say is: "I am
bound to attend Mass; whether I was right or
wrong, whether I am cross or happy, I will
go." It is better to go even with angry feelings, and avoid the sin of losing Mass, than to
stay away.

Depend upon it, if you act on this principle,
before you reach the church your resentment
will begin to disappear. A few words of
prayer: "God, help me"; "Jesus, teach me";
"My Mother Mary, pray for me," will set
everything right again; and the very spirit of
the humble Jesus, the Lamb of God, will fill
you with consolation.

In all our troubles, afflictions, trials, risings
of passion or temptations, the surest help is to
have recourse to God in the church, and especially in time of Holy Mass. Bend your whole
heart to the performance of this duty.

This command to assist at Mass must not be
misunderstood. It is different from the Com-

mandments that forbid blasphemy, impurity, dishonesty, and such like things. These are evil in themselves, and can never be lawful. But the obligation to hear Mass may be taken away by a good and sufficient reason, as I have said already.

In many places and situations it will not be possible to go every Sunday. In the country where there is no church it may happen that we cannot go except rarely. When you do your best, and would gladly go always if you could, God will accept the will for the deed.

Oftentimes the hermits, who served God in the desert, could not hear Mass for a long time; still they grew dearer to God and holier every day. St. Mary of Egypt for many a long year had to forego the happiness of hearing Mass, yet she became a wonderful saint, filled with the spirit of God.

In cases where you cannot attend Mass, endeavor to join yourself, by your prayers, to those who do. Keep your soul quiet and recollected more that day than any other. Keep your room, if you can, a part of the day, read something pious, and I assure you God will make up to you all you would have gained by hearing the Mass.

But, if you have the chance, attend Vespers. Our Lord is present in the Blessed Sacrament; you can at that time adore Him, and pour out your soul before Him. Although it is not so binding a duty as to hear Mass, it is a great help to the soul to attend to it. Every girl who is anxious to give her heart to God, will go to Vespers as well as Mass if she has the opportunity. It is a solemn service of the Church, and a great blessing attends its observance. Ah! we need as much grace as we can get to keep our hearts fixed on God. Is it not better to be in his house than to be gadding about, and losing in idle talk the good influences which the day is expected to leave behind it?

Morning and evening, let us not begrudge to give to God our praise and thanksgiving; then we shall be able with more satisfied minds to enjoy innocent conversation and recreation, a walk, or a visit to friends or relations, at other times of the day.

CHAPTER XIX.

HOW TO ASSIST AT MASS.

" HOW shall I spend my time at Mass? It seems sometimes so long, I do not know what to do. My mind is filled with distractions?"

It is a simple matter to attend at Mass. You come to worship God and to pray. No particular way of doing so is laid down. Each

one is free to do those things that come most
natural to him. Some say the Rosary, and
occupy their minds with good thoughts while
they do so. Others have a book with prayers
for Mass, which they follow; all this is very
well. Others get to understand the meaning
of the different parts of the Mass, and they
follow the Holy Sacrifice better with such
prayers as they find in their own hearts.

For example, at the '' Confiteor '' they strike
their breasts with the priest, and are sorry for
all their sins, and make acts of contrition. At
the '' Offertory,'' when the bread and wine are
offered to God to be used in the Sacrifice, they
offer themselves body, soul, memory, will, and
understanding, all that they are, all, that they
have, and all that they hope for, to God, that
He may do what He pleases with them ; and
determining that all shall be devoted to Him,
and used in his service. All this will take up
a good deal of time, and be very profitable.

When the bell is rung the first time, that is,
at the '' Sanctus,'' they can begin to think
more especially of God, of His greatness and
goodness, of His majesty and love, and their
own lowness and meanness in comparison.
This will bring them along to the '' Elevation,''
when the Holy Host and the Chalice, our Lord
Jesus Christ Himself, is elevated or raised on
high by the priest. Then they can simply

bend down their bodies, and their souls at the same time, in a simple, profound, deep act of worship and adoration of God, who is elevated on high on purpose to receive it. After the elevation we can prepare for the "Communion" that follows, when the priest receives the most Precious Body and Blood.

If you do not "receive" at the Mass, at least you may do what you would do if you were going to receive. You can say with the priest: "Lord, I am not worthy." You can beg the Lord to visit your heart. You can ask the same graces as if you did receive; then you can thank Him for all His goodness, and all that He has done for you, which will occupy your time until the close of the Mass.

Now, is not this a good way to hear Mass? It seems to me that it should come natural to everybody. I am confident that many among educated people prefer this way to any other. They shut up their books, and let their souls have free liberty to raise themselves as they find most natural and most fitted to promote the love of God; the end and object of all devotion. Pious thoughts, good desires, and prayers of every sort, and in any order, will suffice to make the hearing of Mass profitable.

Returning home from church after an hour thus devoutly spent, I am sure you will not forget the sacred character of the day, nor go into

places dangerous to your soul, nor keep any
evil company. The same modesty and recol-
lection you brought from church will attend
you everywhere, and when night comes around
you will be ready to exclaim before you retire
to rest: "What a happy and useful day I have
spent!" "One day in thy courts is better
than a thousand. It is better to be a door-
keeper in the house of my God, than to dwell
in the tents of the ungodly" (Ps. lxxxiii. 10).
With a light, cheerful heart you will commend
your soul to God, now prepared with good
courage to fight the good fight of faith against
all the enemies of your salvation for the coming week.

CHAPTER XX.

OF READING GOOD BOOKS.

IT will frequently happen that you will have
leisure time at your disposal. When the
work of the day is over in the afternoon, in the
long evenings of winter, and especially on Sundays, the time will be your own, and you can do
what you like with it. And it will be a happy
thing for you if you pass it so as to increase the
spirit of devotion.

But you feel tired, perhaps, and unable to
pray. We cannot always be on our knees, we

cannot always think, and it is not the Lord's will that we should overdo anything, not even prayer.

Now, there is a beautiful and easy way of spending one's time piously, and of keeping up at the same time the spirit of prayer. That way consists in the reading of good books. We need to be entertained and to have amusement sometimes, that our minds may not get too worried and unable to think clearly and rightly.

The conversation of a good friend is very pleasant; it gives us this amusement without doing us any harm, and oftentimes it does us a great deal of good. Now, a good book is a good friend. The pages, it is true, do not look at us and smile in our faces; they do not talk to us with all those sweet tones of a friend's voice; they do not talk aloud, but still they do talk to us. They give us many new ideas, they instruct us in many things we did not know before—indeed, they can make us laugh and make us weep. Who can read the happy death of a saint without feeling the tears start from his eyes?

Books are, next to sermons, next to the living voice of the preacher, the most powerful means to excite us to virtue. Get, then, at least a few books, and read them when you get a chance.

"Oh!" says a good girl, "I wish I could! I have never been taught to read, and am now

too old to learn ; besides, I have no opportunity
for learning ; there is no one to teach me, and I
haven't the time.''

Now, do not be cast down on that account.
There is one beautiful book, at least, we can
read ; and that is the Crucifix.   What fountains
of knowledge and true wisdom it contains ! You
can look at it, and think over what it means,
from one year's end to another, yet you will
never reach the bottom of it.

St. Bonaventure, who wrote so many beauti-
ful things, was asked where he got them all ?
What books he had learned them out of ?
'' There is my book,'' said he, pointing to the
Crucifix ; '' all my knowledge, all my thoughts
come from that.''

Another lovely book you have that you can
read, though you never learned a letter of the
alphabet, and that is the Rosary.   Millions who
could not read a word have read that book
every day.   Get some one to teach you the
meaning of the mysteries, and you will never
fail to have the best of books always at hand.
There is no need, then, to be cast down because
you cannot read ; only keep your heart simply
directed to God, and he will make up abundantly for all that is lacking.   Many of the
saints have not been able to read, but they could
pray, and think of Christ's sufferings and love
for them, wonderfully well.

"But why say a word about those who cannot read, since they cannot read what you
say?" That is true; but somebody else may
read it to them, or tell them, and then my object will be accomplished, which is to give every
one such instruction and consolation as is necessary for them.

If you can read, then it is the Lord's will
that you should make use of this gift; for He
requires us to make good use of all our talents
and opportunities. "To whom much is given,
of him much will be required" (St. Luke
xii. 48).

CHAPTER XXI.

OF READING THE BIBLE.

YOU need not, however, have a great many
books; a few good ones are all-sufficient to
furnish food for your souls. Such books can be
read over and over without getting tired of
them. They will always renew some good impression, and excite in you a strong desire to
regulate your life so as to please God better.
There is one book far above all others that have
ever been written or ever will be—that is, the
Holy Bible. This book is different from all
other books, because we can put the most entire

confidence in all that is written in it. Why?
It is God Himself, the Holy Ghost, that has
caused it to be written for our benefit. This is
what the Scripture itself says: "All Scripture,
divinely inspired, is profitable to teach, to re-
prove, to correct, to instruct in justice, that the
man of God may be perfect, furnished unto
every good work" (2 Tim. iii. 16).

Especially is this the case with the New Testament, which is better fitted to our times and
circumstances, which is for the most part plainer and easier to be understood, and which tells
us all that has been done for us by our Saviour
and His apostles.

In the Old Testament, I would advise you to
select such parts as you can read with understanding and profit, and not those which are
above your comprehension, or not applicable to
your situation. There are many prophecies,
and accounts of ceremonies, and some narra-
tives, which, though edifying, no doubt, to
those who understand them, are only curious and
without profit to those who do not. Such things
are better let alone. Perhaps some person
who is acquainted with the different books will
advise you what to read, and what not.

In the New Testament it is different. Every
part of it is full of holy instruction, and I am
not at all afraid that any harm will come to a
well-intentioned, pure-minded person, from read-

ing it; on the contrary, such persons will not fail to derive much good from it.

But does not St. Peter say, speaking of the epistles of St. Paul and the other Scriptures, that in them "are many things hard to be understood which the unlearned and the unstable wrest to their own perdition?" (2 Peter iii. 16). Undoubtedly he does, and nothing can be more true. There are even things which seem perfectly plain and easy to understand, that would certainly mislead any but a scholar unless they were explained. Such things were understood well enough at the time they were written, because all the people were accustomed to use words in the sense in which the writers meant to use them. But now that language and manners have changed, these words have lost the meaning they had at that time, and convey a very different one to us. They must be explained or we shall be misled.

Other things are very deep and difficult in themselves, even to scholars, and it is a real folly to set up one's opinion about them without an explanation.

It is the Church's office to guard and preserve the true sense of the Scripture, as you remember the Scripture itself calls her "the pillar and ground of the truth." The Church, where the meaning of a passage is obscure, or has become changed in the translation from one language to another, has placed notes and explanations to preserve the original meaning. There can be no objection to reading a Catholic Bible, and I find it strongly recommended to the faithful as the best of all books to read. Pope Pius VI. declares that "the faithful should be excited to read the Holy Scriptures, which are the most abundant fountains to be left open to every one to draw from them purity of morals and doctrine," and he declares that "this is most suitably effected by publishing the sacred writings in the language of the country, suited to every one's capacity, with suitable explanations." (See beginning of Catholic Bible.)

It is true the proud and the evil-minded can injure themselves by the reading, but what of that? Cannot everything good be turned into evil by such persons? I have seen self-conceited and ignorant people do this, and to the great peril of their salvation. Were the matter not so serious, one could not help laughing at the absurd sense sometimes put on the Scripture by such people. Could they have either a little more learning or a little more sense, they would see what others see so plainly, how utterly ridiculous they have made themselves. Read, then, the Catholic Bible in the proper spirit, not for disputation or display of learning, but for the good of your soul.

CHAPTER XXII.

CONTINUATION.

BUT do not read or keep in your possession a Protestant Bible or Testament. "Whoever," says our Lord, "is not with me, is against me" (St. Matt. xii. 30). This Bible is not authorized by the holy Church, the guardian of the Scripture. That should be enough to condemn it in the eyes of Catholics; for what confidence can we have in a book that has passed out of the keeping of God's Church into that of men who have no authority, and who do with it what their own judgment and their own light dictate?

The Protestant translation is different from the Catholic in many places, and is generally thrown out on the world without any explanation; as they say, "without note or comment." It becomes then a book that "the unlearned and the unstable are likely to wrest to their own perdition," as St. Peter says. If it has any explanations, they are made by Protestants, too often in order to bolster up their own false religion, by covering up and destroying the real truth. A true child of God will not, then, either keep it or read it.

Girls who are living out may find some mistresses who are all on fire to draw you away from your holy faith. They have an idea that the best way to do it is to get you first to read the Protestant Bible, and by and by they will volunteer to explain it in their own way. They come with smiling faces and coaxing words and say, "I have taken a great fancy to you, and think a great deal of you. I want to make you a little present. Here is a beautiful copy of the Bible." Then they show it, all bound with red morocco, with gilt edges, and perhaps adorned with pictures. "Isn't it beautiful? Take it, my dear, and read it. It cannot hurt you. It is the Word of God, and full of good things." The poor girl is so overwhelmed at this that she does not know what to reply. She takes it and thanks the giver.

Another girl, with a little more courage, will make out to say, "I am much obliged to you, ma'am, but I would rather not take it." "And why not? Are you afraid to read the Scripture, the Word of God? I have heard that Catholics were afraid to read the Bible, but I did not believe it. Yes, I see! the priests are afraid to let you read the Bible lest you find out the errors of your religion." This poor girl feels abashed; she is not used to be attacked in that way, and she perhaps says, "No, ma'am, it is not as you suppose. I will take the book, much obliged to you."

Now, this is just what the lady wanted, to make you do something contrary to your faith, to undermine its firmness, to get some kind of acknowledgment out of you that, after all, the Protestant religion has the truth as well as the Catholic. She hopes, when you begin to waver, you will keep on until you lose the faith altogether.

Let me put in your mind a reply to all such attacks. Say, "I thank you for your good intention, but I cannot accept your book." "Why not? Are you forbid to read the Bible?" "Oh no! I am very glad to read it; but I cannot read any but the true Bible— the Catholic Bible. If you will present me with a copy of that, I will read it, and feel obliged to you for your kindness."

And what is true of the Protestant Bible is true also of other Protestant books, treating of piety or religious doctrine. They may seem to read well and to contain good principles. I have no doubt they do contain some; it would be strange enough if they did not. But there are also evil ones concealed among the good, and the piety is of a false and injurious character. "Beware," says the Saviour, "of false prophets who come in sheep's clothing, but inwardly they are ravenous wolves" (St. Matthew vii. 15).

The mild and gentle Saviour said this because He knew how destructive false doctrine is to the soul, and He would tell the truth, whether every one liked it or not. I have no intention to offend any one, but I must tell the truth, and therefore I tell you to have nothing to do with any religious books not of God's church, neither read them, keep them, nor give them away to anybody else.

CHAPTER XXIII.

HOW TO READ THE BIBLE.

HAVING seen what is to be avoided in the reading of the Scripture, let us speak a little more of the advantage of it. It is a mine of gold to the soul. You have heard, perhaps, how the miners in California work for gold— how they dig day after day, in water and deep under the ground, where they are liable to be crushed to death by the falling of the soil. If they chance to find a large lump of gold, they esteem all their hardships as nothing; they are ready to leap and dance for the joy of their hearts.

But a single verse of Holy Scripture is oftentimes of more value to the immortal soul than all the gold of the world for the body. St. Anthony, the hermit, when a young man, entered a church one day when the Holy Scripture was being read. He heard the words, "Go, sell all that thou hast and give to the poor, and come follow me '' (St. Luke xviii. 22). They sunk right down into his soul. He obeyed them, sold his possessions, gave the money to the poor, and went into the desert, that he might follow the Lord Jesus Christ more perfectly. There he became one of the greatest of saints.

How many places there are that fill us with hope, with consolation, with strong desire to serve God. Why, we can think over a single sentence for months and months, and even our whole lives, and constantly find matter for thought and prayer. Take that beautiful sermon of our Lord on the mount; who can ever understand the whole perfection of it? or who could fail to find something in it to feed his soul, if he were to read it over every week of his life?

I was much pleased with an expression I found in the lives of some nuns who lived in the time of St. Basil, fourteen hundred years ago. It is said ''they nourished their souls with the daily food of the divine Scriptures.'' That is, they meditated them over, and set themselves to work at once to carry out their teachings as well as they could. And the good people of those times who could not read listened with all their ears to hear the Holy Scriptures, counting themselves as rich if they could remember one verse to carry away with them, as if a precious pearl had been given them.

If we were as docile and as watchful, what a treasure we should find in the Scriptures! Read them with attention, with the wish always to get good out of them. Do not run over too much at one time; but, when something strikes you, pause over it, think over it, and lift your heart to God, to beg Him to fix it in your soul, to thank Him for the good thoughts and feelings which come to you, or to make other prayers, as you may feel inclined. And afterward try to keep it in your mind, so that you may be able to call it back when you like. It will help you to pray with fervor.

I like this mixing of reading and prayer; and when your reading excites prayer, by all means stop, raise your eyes or close them, and pray as long as you feel inclined to. Then go on with your reading. Maybe in a very short time some other good thought will strike you, and you will want to pray again. Do so; and do not be afraid to interrupt the reading as often as you have something to say to God.

This is the way St. Teresa used to do, and she became, as is well known, the very saint to teach others how to pray. She helped herself with a book, just in the way I have described, until finally she needed no book, for she could hardly help praying all the time, it became so natural to her.

CHAPTER XXIV.

OF OTHER GOOD BOOKS.

IF you had no other book than the New Testament, it would be an abundance of good reading. Still, it is well to have a little variety. Any good book of instructions, such as the *Mission Book*, is of great advantage, because there you will find what you most want to know laid out in order, and in such a way that you can understand it. The Scripture excites you to do right in general; but such a book teaches you how to carry out the teaching of the Scripture, and to regulate your life in practice; how to behave under the actual circumstances of life, so that you need not fear being led astray through want of knowing what to do.

St. Philip Neri was once asked what books he thought the best. He replied, those whose writers' names begin with an S. That is, those written by the *saints*, by men or women filled with the spirit of God. There are many beautiful books written by such persons; for instance, the works of St. Francis of Sales and of St. Alphonsus Liguori. Choose among these a few that suit your taste, but do not be anxious to get too many.

There is one book which I think very good for daily reading during the year, and that is, Butler's *Lives of the Saints.* We feel so much encouraged to press on in the way of virtue, and to follow the Saviour, when we read how others have done so before us. In this excellent work are the lives of the principal saints, with many good instructions and observations which explain what otherwise might be misunderstood.

It was by reading the lives of the saints that St. Ignatius was excited to a holy life. He had been wounded in battle, and was laid up a long time before he recovered. The time hung heavy on his hands, and to occupy his mind he read all the novels he could get. When there were no more, they brought him some lives of the saints. Soon after he began to read, their earnestness and courage in striving for the Kingdom of Heaven touched his heart. "Why cannot I do likewise?" said he; and immediately he began to give himself up heart and soul, with all his energy, to serve God.

These moving and affecting lives may touch your hearts too, and urge you on to do your whole duty with courage and perseverance. Only be careful not to attempt rashly to imitate them in those things that are extraordinary and

singular, such as great fasting or bodily austeri-
ties. The humility, the meekness and patience
of the saints, their love to one another—these
things you can safely follow, the more closely
the better. But their extraordinary works of
penance were performed through a particular
inspiration of the Holy Ghost, and it would be
both unwise and injurious for ordinary persons
to undertake them. Leave all that is wonderful and unusual. These things we can admire,
but must not be too quick to imitate.

But above all, put out of your heads the wish
to see visions, or to have miracles performed by
God for you, or to dream dreams, or any things
of the sort. When God sends them it is all
well. It is not probable, however, that He will
send them, and it is not pleasing to Him if we
ask for them or desire them. It would be much
better to say, "O my God! I am content to
walk by the simple light of faith. If it be Thy
will, please preserve me from all dreams, visions, or any extraordinary ways, and let me
sanctify myself by doing my duty and Thy
blessed will in all things."

The devil has no chance to deceive the soul
that walks in this road, and her humility will
draw down God's richest graces.

Read, then, and pray, and what the Scripture
says of the just man will be true of you: "His
will is the law of the Lord, and in His law he

shall meditate day and night. And he shall be like a tree planted near the running water, which produces its fruit in due season, for its leaf shall not fall. And behold, whatever he doeth shall prosper '' (Psalm i.) Be faithful to these holy exercises, and you will be watered abundantly by the divine grace, grow steadily and rapidly in goodness, and produce in due time the fruits of holiness. Everything will turn out well for your soul, until you shall reap your blessed reward in heaven.

CHAPTER XXV.

ON THE NATURE OF THE SACRAMENTS.

OF all the means of leading a devout life, the most important remain yet to be spoken of. These are the holy Sacraments of Penance and the Eucharist, or, as they are commonly called, of Confession and Communion.

There are, as you know, other sacraments besides these, but I only wish to speak here of these two because they are to be received frequently, and are adapted to the every-day wants of the soul.

These may be called the very means of our Lord Jesus Christ Himself, since He established them to remain until the end of the world, in order to impart to us the graces necessary to bring us to everlasting life.

You know our Lord is represented in the Gospel as the Good Shepherd, who watches over His flock to keep all harm away from it, and to provide it with the best and most agreeable nourishment. I have seen most affecting pictures, in which He is represented carrying the poor stray sheep on His shoulders safe home to the fold. Now, it is especially through the holy sacraments that our Lord fulfils this office of Shepherd of our souls.

Through them He guards us from the enemies who are on the look-out to surprise and destroy us. Through them He gives us food for the soul that makes us strong and healthful, and full of courage, and through them He gives the sweetest consolation in all our distress and down-heartedness.

These sacraments are not merely something within us, that passes between our soul and God, but they are outward signs, something that we see or hear or do—as, for example, when we wish to receive the Sacrament of Penance, we not only prepare ourselves in our hearts, but we go to the priest of God, we declare to him our sins, and he raises his hand and pronounces the Absolution over us.

To these outward and visible signs our Blessed Saviour has joined wonderful though hidden graces, which produce silently and quietly the greatest effects on our souls. What a consolation this is! To know by the sure words of the Saviour, that when with true, sincere hearts we receive these sacraments, we receive those precious graces which are attached to them. Our very eyes and ears in this way become witnesses to our happiness. For they tell us that the actions have been performed, or the words spoken, to which our faith assures us that the Lord has given a divine grace and power.

Perhaps you can understand this better by a comparison. Suppose a generous-hearted rich man to have made the acquaintance of a poor family. He likes them, and seeing that they are well-meaning, honest people, determines to give them a house to live in, and a little garden around it. So he brings out pen and ink and paper, and writes out a deed, then signs and seals it, and the property becomes theirs. What joy and gratitude fill their hearts when they see this deed with the good man's name and seal upon it, assuring them that the property is really theirs!

So the things that are done or said in Confession and Communion, like the signing of the deed, assure us that a great property, a glorious possession for the soul, has become ours. The Lord has promised it, and these outward ceremonies are the signing and sealing which convey the title to us. Blessings and praises, then, be to our Lord for these glorious sacraments which He has left behind Him in His holy Church!

CHAPTER XXVI.

CONFESSION A REMEDY FOR SIN.

THE Sacrament of Confession was instituted by our Lord for the forgiveness of sin. Nothing can be more important for us than this sacrament, if we have fallen into sin. It is sin that bars the gates of heaven. With mortal or grievous sin on the conscience, we are, as Scripture says, already condemned; and the sentence is only removed when the sin is forgiven. Sin is the thing to be feared above all else. Great or grievous sins kill the soul outright. If they are not destroyed by penance and forgiven, we must suffer the pains of hell for them. Every kind of sin, whether small or great, is exceedingly to be feared. A venial sin, particularly such as is deliberately committed—that is, committed with the knowledge and consciousness that it is a sin —helps to destroy the soul. It may seem to be a small matter, but it weakens the love of God in the soul, and if persevered in paves the way for greater ones, until, little by little, one falls entirely.

I wish I could impress this upon your minds so that you might never forget it. Our Blessed

Saviour was always urging this point; always declaring that the sin must be abandoned if we expect to please God or be saved. "Fear not those that kill the body," He says, "and cannot kill the soul: but rather fear Him that can destroy both soul and body in hell." What is that for which God will destroy the soul? It is sin. And sin alone can.

The Pharisees are described as making long prayers, and going through all the observances of the Law with the utmost exactness, expecting in this way to satisfy God, though they kept on committing sin. Just see how our Lord denounces them.

"Woe to you Scribes and Pharisees, hypocrites, because you are like to whited sepulchres, which outwardly appear to men beautiful: but within are full of dead men's bones and all filthiness. So you also outwardly, indeed, appear to men just: but within you are full of hypocrisy and iniquity."

"Woe to you Scribes and Pharisees, because you devour the houses of widows, making long prayers; therefore you shall receive the greater judgment." "You serpents, generation of vipers, how will you escape the judgment of hell?" (St. Matt. xxiii. 14, 27, 28, 33).

I am afraid this description will apply to some Catholics. I am afraid there are some girls who have an idea that if they have some outward devotion, if they go to church and pray there, and go to the sacraments now and then, they need not be so particular to avoid sin.

Sometimes you hear an employer say: "There is my girl; she is on her knees praying a great deal, but in five minutes after flies into such a rage that you would think her possessed of the devil. She goes to her confession, but the next day you will hear words out of her mouth that would disgrace a heathen."

Another says: "Mary attends church and says her prayers, but she pilfers and takes things that do not belong to her: she wastes a great deal of time, and does her work in the most careless and slovenly manner. She does not seem to understand that the first principle of religion requires her to be honest and fulfil her duty to her employers."

Now, what kind of religion is that? Such girls grossly deceive themselves, but they do not and cannot deceive the Almighty. "If ye love me, keep my commandments"; that is, do not sin. Do not think that anything else can be put in the place of really and truly keeping the commandments of God. Remember the words of the Holy Ghost: "Flee from sin as from the face of a serpent" (Ecclus. xxi. 2). Flee from sin: hate sin; have a horror and dread of sin; and make it the study of your life to avoid every sin, and every appearance of sin.

CHAPTER XXVII.

CONTINUATION.

NOW, the Sacrament of Penance, or Confession, is the grand remedy for sin. It is the medicine of the Saviour, established to heal the wounds of the soul—the great cure for all its sicknesses. When we make a good Confession, and the priest pronounces over us the Absolution, or sentence of forgiveness, our sins are forgiven. Nor is this all: Confession cleanses the heart, and inspires us with a hatred of sin. All that we do to prepare for it has a tendency to make us see the hateful nature of sin, and in the sacrament itself the grace of God confirms this hatred in us in a remarkable way.

The power of this sacrament comes from the words of Christ Himself. He gave to His priests, in the most solemn way, the commission to forgive sins, saying: "As my father hath sent me, so I send you. Receive ye the Holy Ghost. Whose soever sins you remit, they shall be remitted unto them; and whose soever sins you retain, they shall be retained" (St. John xx. 23).

Some one may say to you: "God alone can forgive sins. Why do you go to a priest, or to

any man, and not directly to God?'' I answer:
'' True, God alone has the power to forgive sins ;
but it is by God's power that the priest forgives
sins, and not by any power of his own. Why
do I not go to God directly for forgiveness rather
than to the priest? Because He has committed
His power to the priest, and told me to go to
him.'' For the same reason that I pay my fare
to the conductor and not to the president of a
railroad : he is the one delegated to receive it.

It is not for me to set up my own notion in
place of God's ordinance. When God said to
the priest: '' Whose sins ye forgive they are forgiven,'' that is enough for me. When I know
the road He has told me to travel, it is not for
me to turn off from it, no matter how flattering
or pleasant any other way may appear. It will
be very bitter at the day of judgment, after having gone astray from following our own notions,
to hear our Lord's reproach : '' Why were you
not satisfied with My way—the way that in My
infinite wisdom I saw best for you? and why did
you, in your short-sighted wisdom, set up another in place of it ? ''

The priest is a man, it is true ; but he is the
agent of the Lord Jesus Christ. All his acts,
within the limits of the commission or agency
committed to him, will be held good by his
Lord. If he steps out of that he is no longer an
agent, and his Lord will not hold such acts good.

It is like any other agency, and the same principles govern it.

Therefore, when the priest exercises his ministry of mercy and reconciliation, he applies the blood and merits of the Saviour to the penitent for the washing away of sins. When he absolves, it is the Holy Ghost that absolves through his means, washes us clean with Christ's most precious blood, and confirms us in God's holy love. Hence, after Confession, sin seems to have lost its hold on our affections, and the devil is afraid to bring forward his temptations for some time, lest he be driven back in disgrace.

CHAPTER XXVIII.

WE MUST NOT PUT OFF THE USE OF THIS REMEDY.

CONFESSION being thus the remedy for sin, we ought thankfully and diligently to make use of it; but the devil raises up great difficulties in the way, sometimes deterring sinners from approaching this sacrament of which they stand in the greatest need; sometimes tormenting the good who do approach it with so many scruples as to deprive them of a great part of its benefit.

There are persons who are conscious to themselves that they are living in the state of mortal

sin, and who desire to get out of it, and to re-
cover the grace of God, but who are frightened
at the idea that it is so very difficult a thing to
do. "How shall I examine my conscience,"
they say, "when I have committed so many
sins? I can never recollect them in the world.
I cannot go through with them."

Now, all these difficulties are purely in the
imagination. Set yourself at the work with a
simple, childlike intention to go through it well,
and all the difficulties will disappear. If you
resolve to make a sincere, honest confession,
with heartfelt sorrow and a firm determination to
quit your sins and live a good life afterwards, all
the trouble about Confession will vanish like
smoke before the wind.

As to the impossibility of calling your numerous sins to mind, I say a few days of preparation
will be sufficient for a confession of a life-time,
even though it has been filled with sins. Fervent prayers to God from the heart, with now
and then a look at your past life, will bring up,
little by little, all that is important to be confessed.

If you are unable to apply your mind, a good
will, and a desire to please God, will draw down
grace from Him to do all that he requires of
you.

Besides, your confessor will give you the
benefit of his experience, and make the difficulty

very slight. Be humble and sorrowful for sin, and determined to quit it, and your confessor will feel obliged to help you, or rather to co-operate with God in that great work that He is carrying on in your soul. You will be surprised when you have finished your confession to see how very easy it has been, and you will be in-clined to say : "How is it possible that my lov-ing Saviour can accomplish such wonderful things for me, when I have done so little my-self!"

Do not follow the example of some girls, who go year after year with a guilty conscience, and when asked, "Why have you not been to your confession before?" reply : "I had stayed away so long I was afraid to come"; or, "I felt there was such a load upon me, that I had not the courage to throw it off"; or, "I was afraid the priest would scold me for being so neglectful." Nonsense! nonsense! the whole of this is non-sense. It is the devil trying to fill your mind full of fancies in order to hinder you from doing a good thing, a pleasant thing, a delightful and easy thing.

You have suffered, perhaps, untold agony of mind, and carried a big burden which you could have thrown off whenever you pleased. The same amount of trouble you have taken a hun-dred times in your worldly affairs, had it been given to God, would have been sufficient to have relieved you entirely. Jesus Christ would at once have taken all that guilt away from you, had you only applied to Him in the way that He has prescribed.

CHAPTER XXIX.

EXAMPLE OF ST. MARY OF EGYPT.

FOR the consolation of all who may be troubled with such fears, and to confirm what I have said, let me give you the example of St. Mary of Egypt. This great saint, who attained to such a wonderful purity of heart and astonishing sanctity in her old age, was in her youth quite as remarkable for the wickedness and vileness of her life. From the age of twelve, for sixteen years, she was a scandal and offence to the Christian name by her abominable life. In the midst of her career of wickedness she saw one day a number of pilgrims taking ship for Jerusalem, to visit the holy places which our Lord had sanctified by His life and precious death.

She determined to join herself to the company, not from any pious motive but in order to carry on her wickedness with more facility. When the ship arrived, the pilgrims went up to the church to venerate the Holy Cross on which the

Saviour died, and Mary, all hardened and wicked as she was, went up with the rest.

With bold face she was pushing in at the door, but an invisible power stopped her short at the threshold. Do what she could, she could not enter. She went away and came back to try again, but it was of no use. She was filled with fear, and the grace of God entered her heart. She recognized her own vileness and sinfulness, and tears began to flow down her cheeks.

She turned to the Blessed Virgin, whose statue was placed at the entrance of the church, and said : " O Holy Virgin, mother of the Word made flesh, so pure and humble and chaste, intercede for me. Procure for me, a vile creature, the grace to go in and venerate the Holy Cross on which thy Son shed His blood, and I promise no more to return to my bad life, but to do penance in any way that may be most pleasing to God."

Her prayer was heard, and she found afterwards no difficulty in entering and venerating the Holy Cross. Then, her heart filled with contrition, she commenced the penance which God the Holy Ghost inspired her to do, in order to make amends for her sins and establish herself in His fear and love.

That very day she started for the desert country beyond the river Jordan. She arrived at nightfall at the bank of the river, where there was a church of St. John the Baptist. Now notice what follows : she received Holy Communion that day. Her sighs and tears and prayers, as she travelled along the road, had prepared her. The enormity of her life was before her in all its dark colors. With simplicity of heart, and the single thought of declaring her sin the best she could, so as to forsake it for ever, she made her confession.

It was enough : she told her sins as well as she could ; she answered her confessor with simplicity, and her confession was finished. There was no need to tell her to come again. It was made just as well that once as if she had come back twenty times, and better.

" But maybe she was a very learned woman, who had been so well instructed that she knew how to make her confession perfectly." Such was not the case. It was quite the contrary. She could not read a word, and seems to have been a very ignorant person, as we may well suppose her to have been, considering how careless and sinful she had been from a small girl up to the time of her conversion.

No : her example shows how ready God is to give sinners abundant grace to make a good confession, and to remove every difficulty when He sees a good will. " But did not St. Mary get so scrupulous that she had to repeat over her confession afterwards a number of times ? " Not

at all.   She lived in the desert fifty-seven years
in penance and prayer.   Her confidence in
God's goodness and mercy, and her consciousness of her own sincerity, were sufficient to put
away all vain and silly scruples, so that her
peace and tranquillity of soul became almost
angelic.

Any girl who comes to confession with simplicity and earnestness as St. Mary did, no matter how much she may have sinned, will find it
easy, as Mary did, and will receive from God
graces similar to those that Mary received.

Let us thank God for this consoling Sacrament of Penance, and, when we return from it
cleansed and strengthened, say, with the Blessed Virgin : "My soul doth magnify the Lord,
and my spirit exult in God my Saviour, who
hath had regard to the humility of His hand-
maid.   For He who is powerful hath done great
things for me : blessed be His holy name " (St.
Luke i. 46).

CHAPTER XXX.

SCRUPLES OF THE GOOD CONCERNING CONFESSION.

IF the enemy of our souls strives to keep sinners away from Confession by magnifying its difficulties, he endeavors also to discourage and harass the penitent who frequents the Sacrament by groundless fears and scruples.

These scruples and torments are either in reference to the declaration of their sins, or their dispositions in regard to them. Such persons feel so deeply the importance of salvation that they desire to have a certainty about it which is not good for them, nor according to the holy will of God, that they should have.

Though such fears are natural, they must be put aside, and not dwelt upon nor made much of, when they stand in the way of our peace of mind, or the real, genuine love of God. I will say something about them that you may understand their nature, and the folly of them.

There are some who are always tormented lest they should have omitted something in their confessions. They seem to fancy that if by any chance a considerable sin should entirely escape their memories and never come up again, it would remain unforgiven, and appear against them at the judgment. Just as if God, the Infinite Goodness, could ever condemn any one for what was not his own fault! Such an idea is entirely absurd.

No doubt, a good girl when she first begins to enter seriously into God's service will do her best to have a clear conscience, and will not willingly allow any considerable sins to remain unconfessed. But one confession made with such intention is enough to put her in a state of grace, as everything that can hinder God's grace is removed by a sincere and contrite confession.

After such a confession it is God's will that we should be free from all over-anxiety about our salvation, and it is contrary to His will that we should worry and fret, and be troubled in mind. If we have forgotten anything of importance, it does not make us lose God's grace. We should remain in the utmost tranquillity until the next confession, when the forgotten sin can be declared; for although it is forgiven, it is necessary to confess it, if it has not been confessed already.

Again: many give themselves much more anxiety about the examination of their consciences than is necessary. Of course, all grievous sins must be confessed, but a good girl will hate and abhor such sins so much that I suppose she will rarely, if ever, fall into them. I suppose, if she has unfortunately sinned in such a way, that she will immediately enter into herself and grieve over it, and be only too anxious to confess it. As soon as she begins to prepare for confession, it will be uppermost in her mind, and there will be no danger of her forgetting it.

As to smaller sins, our examination of conscience need not be scrupulous and anxious; on the contrary, it ought to be entirely tranquil and peaceful. Think over your sins and faults, and be as sorry for them as you please; that is all very well; but do not imagine that the chief good of confession is in being sure not to leave out anything.

This is not the case. If you are sorry for everything that displeases God, and declare all your grievous sins, and such of the others as you deem most hurtful and injurious, you do well— and better than if your whole mind were set on a minute and particular declaration of every small matter.

Sometimes, while the priest is speaking to you of something very important to your soul, some danger you must avoid, or some practice of piety he sees useful to you, he will be interrupted in the very middle of his advice by something like this: "I neglected my morning prayers sometimes"; or, "I have been out of patience"; or, "I have been fretful."

This is making confession a matter of form,

and forgetting the spirit of it; like the Pharisees of old, who put everything in the most minute observance of the smallest ceremonies, while they paid little attention to really cleansing and purifying their hearts from attachment to sin.

Your time is better employed in sorrow and regret for what is wrong and defective, in holy resolutions to amend your lives, and to give your hearts to God more perfectly, than in a scrupulous and over-anxious examination of conscience.

In the same way, the desire to be constantly repeating over confessions that have been already well made seems to me calculated to do no good, but rather to keep the mind in constant trouble and anxiety, when it ought to be putting a loving trust in God. It is making God ''a hard master,'' exacting to the last farthing, when in truth He is a kind Father and has long ago forgiven us.

There is a secret pride about it, too, as if it were by our own force and strength that we were to look for forgiveness, and not in the loving mercy of God.

CHAPTER XXXI.

SCRUPLES CONCERNING CONTRITION.

MANY good girls are also often troubled about their contrition or sorrow for sin. They fear they have never had the right kind of sorrow, and that their confessions are of no value on that account. I venture to say, that those who fear this very much are the very ones who have no cause to fear. This fear shows a desire to do God's will and a grief at the very idea of not doing it, and what is that but true sorrow for sin?

Contrition does not consist in feeling, for we cannot always feel as we would wish to, but in a firm determination to do God's holy will, and to hate and abhor what is contrary thereto.

Seeing that our sins are contrary to His will, we sincerely regret them; they are a grief to us; we wish most heartily that they had never been committed, and we are determined that they never shall be committed again.

You may seem to yourselves to be cold and without feeling; yet if your contrition is of this kind it is a far better proof of God's being pleased with you than the shedding of a torrent of tears would be.

Tears sometimes flow very lightly and on small occasions, and they dry up quite as readily. The virtue and goodness of religion is not at all in such tears. On the contrary, the deepest and strongest acts of the will are generally those which are the calmest and most tranquil. The noisy brook is very shallow, while the still water runs deep.

When we read of the martyrs of old giving their blood and their life rather than burn incense to false gods, because they knew that this was a sin, we see what an abhorrence they had of sin, and we are sure that they hated their own past sins, and grieved over them with the most sincere contrition. If you in the same way are disposed to deny yourselves all that may be necessary in order to avoid sin, even though it should go much against your inclination—that is, if your will is heartily set against sin—you need have no anxiety about your contrition; you may be sure it is all right.

The best way to be sure of always having a true contrition for your faults, even the slightest, is to exercise yourselves well in constant desires after God's love, as I have already recommended you. You know what the Scripture says: "No man can serve two masters, for either he will love the one and hate the other, or hold to the one and despise the other." If God is truly the master of your soul, there is no fear but you will hate the devil and all his works, and as soon as you see that anything whatever is contrary to the love of God you will drive it from your heart.

If you say : " I won't be impatient as I have been before " ; or, " I will be more careful of my tongue, not to speak in a passion " ; and at the same time do not cherish a warm desire to please God in all things, I fear all your resolutions will soon be forgotten. But keep your heart and soul directed to God, and you will be attentive to guard against these and all other faults.

When you have a very great desire to please your employer you are not apt to forget any part of your duty, and you do it well, but when the desire is wanting, you may make a resolution a hundred times to do this or that, and forget it.

A girl who desires to catch the eye of others by her dress never forgets to look in the glass, nor to arrange her hair or her ornaments. She has no need to make a resolution not to forget these things, for her desire keeps her memory wide awake.

So keep a burning desire to please God in your mind, and your memory will be quick in regard to sin or faults, and your will strong. "His delight is in the law of the Lord, and in His law he will meditate day and night," says the Scripture (Ps. i. 2). Put your delight in loving God, and the thought of His law will be present before you day and night.

CHAPTER XXXII.

WE MUST HAVE THE SPIRIT OF PENANCE.

IN regard to the penance or satisfaction that is imposed in the Sacrament of Confession, I would observe that it should, of course, be done faithfully; but over and above this, we should endeavor to do penance by all the actions of our lives, principally by putting up with the crosses, troubles, trials, and afflictions which God may see fit to send upon us.

We need, all of us, to do penance; for our sins and faults are more than the hairs of our heads, and what is the little penance imposed on us in Confession? A few prayers, a few recitals of the Rosary, a slight deprivation or self-denial. Truly, it keeps up the principle of penance in the sacrament and reminds us solemnly of our duty; but after all how inadequate it is, and out of proportion to the number and greatness of our sins!

God imposes His own penance as He sees fit and good for us. Oh! let us not stand in the way of His designs for us by refusing to accept His penance, by complaining and fretting under it, or by seeking to escape it amid the dissipations and distractions of the world.

How short-sighted we are! God looks upon us with eyes of love and proposes a very precious gift for us, a splendid diamond that shall sparkle for all eternity. It comes in the shape of a trial, an affliction, or a disappointment. All we have to do is to look through it right up to God, who has allowed it to happen, and to say: "Praise and glory be to God in this as in all things." "If we have received good things from God, why shall we not also receive evil?" (Job ii. 10). When we have done so we have united ourselves to Him more closely than we could have done had all happened according to our desire.

Instead, then, of complaining and grumbling at what God permits to befall us, let us be thankful and take it as a sign that he has not forgotten us; but that He is watching over us with all the interest of a father, desiring our salvation, and holding out to us the means of attaining it.

I am convinced that the reason why many souls are lost is, that they will not submit to these penances. Penance is necessary to purify their souls and destroy the evil root of sin in them, but they will have none of it; they go so much on the principle of self-indulgence and self-love that God's love can find no place in them, and God's grace is thrown away on their hard and sterile hearts.

Let us remember always these blessed words spoken by the priest when he imparts the Absolution. He says : " May the Passion and Suffering of our Lord Jesus Christ, the merits of the Blessed Virgin Mary, and of all the saints, and whatsoever good you shall do, or evil you shall suffer, be to you for the remission of your sins, the increase of grace, and the reward of eternal glory."   The sufferings of this life work out for us, if taken in the spirit of penance, what St. Paul calls " an eternal weight of glory."

Take, then, with patience and joy everything disagreeable, everything painful, everything against your will, the loss of friends, or of property, or of health, or anything whatever as a penance for your sins, from the hands of Jesus Christ, as a filling up of what is wanting in your sacramental penance, and you will be rewarded for it.   It will give you a foretaste of heaven even now in your soul, and heaven itself hereafter.

These are the chief things regarding the Sacrament of Penance which I have deemed it more especially useful to say to you. As to other matters, which may be of equal importance, you will find them sufficiently explained in your prayer-books, or books of instruction, such as the *Mission Book.* Many of you, no doubt, have learned them in your catechisms when you were children. Let us now consider some of the things in regard to Holy Communion which it will be most pleasing and profitable for us thoroughly to understand and to apply to our souls.

CHAPTER XXXIII.

WHAT THE HOLY COMMUNION IS.

THE Holy Communion is the greatest of all the sacraments, because it contains under the appearances of bread and wine the Author of all the sacraments, the Lord Jesus Christ Himself.

Our Lord was not satisfied with giving us the other sacraments, though full of wonderful graces. He determined to put the crowning stone to His work by giving Himself to us. He ascended into heaven, but He is still with us in the Sacrament of the Altar, and will always remain with us until the end of the world.

I dare say you will be pleased to read a short explanation of the way in which our Lord has accomplished such great things.

On the very last night before he suffered death for us on the cross, He and all His Apostles were assembled in an upper room.

They ate their last meal together, and our Saviour conversed with them about all that was to happen to Him. He bade them all farewell in the most affectionate and loving manner, as a father, about to depart on a long and painful journey, would do to his children.

When this was over, He solemnly took bread in His hands and blessed it, and gave it to them, saying these words: " Take, eat; this is My Body." Then He took the cup containing wine, and said: " Drink ye all of this; this is My Blood." When he spake these words, " This is My Body," " This is My Blood," that which He said really became a fact. What He held in His hands became His Body and His Blood. It was bread before, but on speaking the word it was bread no longer; it became His Body. It was wine before, but ceased to be wine at the Lord's word, and became His blood. Such is now the faith of the Church, and such has been the faith in all ages.

Now you may ask: " What is meant by the Body of the Lord, and the Blood of the Lord?" By both these expressions is meant the true, living Body of Christ. That is, the Body of the Lord, together with His Soul and His Divinity. In short, the Lord Himself, perfect and complete. All the qualities of bread and wine, the look, the taste, the smell, remain just as they were before; yet there is no bread and wine;

it is the Lord's Body and Blood, the Lord Himself.

"How can these things be?" That is a question which will be often asked, not by the good Catholic, who believes simply on the word of the Lord, but by those who are strangers to the faith. I do not doubt many a good girl will be asked this question by a Protestant friend or acquaintance.

The answer is: It is by the power of God, who can do all things. We might ask those who put this question: "Please tell me how the Lord of heaven and earth can be contained in the little Babe of Bethlehem, crying and moaning on the straw?" But the Wise Men of the East did not ask the question: "How can it be?" They fell down on their knees and adored Him.

Or, "Tell me how it was that the Lord, with His Flesh and Blood, could pass through the closed doors and appear suddenly among His disciples?" He certainly did so, for they felt the wounds in His hands and in His feet, and found His body as solid and real as that of any other person.

The only answer they can make to these questions is: "It was by His divine, almighty power." Just so; and by the same divine, almighty power He is really and truly in the Sacrament of the Eucharist under the appearances of bread and wine. Hear what St. Cyril of Jerusalem says so beautifully about it: "When He, therefore, pronounced and said of the bread, 'This is My Body,' who shall dare, after that, to doubt? And when He, the very same person, so clearly declared, 'This is My Blood,' who shall ever dare to hesitate to say that it is His Blood? He formerly at Cana of Galilee changed water into wine, which resembles, in some measure, blood, and shall we consider Him unworthy of belief in changing wine into blood?"

But I know every Catholic girl who loves her faith will have the same spirit that St. Jane Frances of Chantal had when she was a little girl. A Protestant gentleman came to her father's house, and in course of conversation ridiculed the doctrine that the Blessed Sacrament is really our Lord's Body. The little girl could not endure this. Indignation filled her heart. The blood reddened her cheeks. "What!" she said, "do you say the Son of God is a liar? Did he not say, 'This is My Body,' and how do you say it is not His Body?" He tried to pacify her by little presents, but she threw them into the fire. "So," she said, "will all burn in the eternal fire who wilfully deny the truth of God's word."

What a blessed thing it is to believe that the Lord of Glory is, as the Council of Trent says, really, truly, and substantially present in the Blessed Sacrament; to believe that we may go to see Him at the altar where He is; that we may lay all our wants before Him, talk with Him, learn to love Him; that he comes to us in Communion at the altar, and is brought to us at our homes to go with us through the pains of sickness and through the valley of the shadow of death.

I do not envy those who do not believe. They rob themselves of the greatest consolation it is possible to have in this dreary and miserable world. "Oh!" said a Protestant minister, not long ago, in a sermon to his people, "if we could only suppose that the Lord was in some way really and bodily present among us as we kneel in the church, how our hearts would leap with joy and glow with a fire of devotion!"

What his heart yearned for, that we know for certain we have in the bosom of the one, holy Catholic Church. Now let us see the effects of the Blessed Sacrament on the soul.

CHAPTER XXXIV.

EFFECTS OF COMMUNION.

THE Lord instituted His Sacrament under the appearance of bread. Why did He choose bread rather than anything else? Because bread is our principal and best food—the staff of life, as it is justly called.

Now, as bread, when it is eaten, is changed into our flesh and blood, and goes through every part of our body to make us strong and well, so the Blessed Sacrament enters the soul, nourishes it, and makes it strong and healthy. As the bread is changed into our flesh and blood to nourish us, so we are changed, in our souls, into Christ.

All the dispositions of our souls become like those of Christ. Everything bad in us is corrected, everything good in us is strengthened. As bread makes the body grow to its full size, so the Blessed Sacrament makes all virtues grow in us until we reach the full measure of holiness that God designs for us.

Without food we should die; the principle of life would not remain in our bodies. So the Lord has said of the Blessed Sacrament: "Except ye eat My Flesh, and drink My Blood, ye shall not have life in you. He that eateth My Flesh and drinketh My Blood hath ever-lasting life, and I will raise him up at the last day: for My Flesh is meat indeed, and My Blood is drink indeed. He who eateth My Flesh and drinketh My Blood abideth in Me, and I in him. As the living Father hath sent Me, and I live by the Father, so he that eateth Me, the same shall also live by Me '' (St. John vi. 54–58).

The Blessed Sacrament is then everything to us. It is the means of keeping the principle of life in the soul ; that everlasting life, unto which body and soul must be preserved until the hour of death !

It is the medicine of the sick soul, tenderly nursing it, and giving it strength against all the dangers that threaten it with death.

How magnificent the simple words of our Lord Jesus, when He began to speak of this sacrament, ''I am the bread of life ! '' Yes, it is He, the Lord of Glory, that comes into our souls in the sacrament, to be the bread of life to us. What may we not ask of Him when He comes ? what may we not expect to receive ? The All-Powerful, the All-Good comes to and visits our souls on purpose to do us good, able to do everything, willing to do everything ; with unspeakable love, desiring to do everything for us.

O dearest handmaids of the Lord! with what desire and love you should long to receive Holy Communion! If you want to form an idea of the benefits of receiving Holy Communion, consider the beautiful little example related in the Gospel of St. Matthew of the woman who was healed of the issue of blood. I cannot do better than use the very words of Scripture: " And behold a woman who was troubled with an issue of blood twelve years, came behind Him and touched the hem of His garment; for she said within herself: 'If I shall but touch His garment I shall be healed.' But Jesus turning around and seeing her, said : ' Take courage, daughter, thy faith hath made thee whole.' And the woman was made whole from that hour " (St. Matt. ix. 20, 21, 22).

The poor woman expected great things from merely touching the garment of Jesus. She was not deceived. What may we not expect, devoutly receiving the same Jesus into our souls?

CHAPTER XXXV.

PREPARATION FOR COMMUNION.

THE foregoing example explains also the spirit in which we should prepare ourselves for Holy Communion. Many have an idea that the proper preparation consists in saying many prayers out of a prayer-book, or going through the various acts of faith, hope, charity, and contrition which they find laid down for the purpose.

This is all very well if those acts are made at the same time with the heart; that is, with real, genuine sincerity, knowing what they mean, and meaning to do what they say. Merely reciting them over, with the idea that this is all that is required, is a very poor preparation indeed.

They may be read over with some feeling, and yet we may not have a sincere disposition to love God and keep His commandments. One may have no disposition to amend his faults, may even think that this feeling good a little while until after Communion is over is enough, and will leave him free to live a life of sin until he sets to work to feel good again, in order to prepare for another Communion.

False piety of this kind is an abomination in

the eyes of God. "This people honoreth Me with their lips, while their heart is far from Me" (St. Matt. xv. 8).

The true preparation for Communion consists, first, in being in a state of grace; or, in other words, being free from mortal sin. To receive Communion knowingly in the state of mortal sin is a sacrilege, or unworthy treatment of the Holy Sacrament—a very grievous sin itself—for, as the Holy Ghost says: " What fellowship can there be between justice and injustice?" (2 Cor. vi. 14).

How can God come into the heart which belongs to Satan? This is what the holy Apostle, St. Paul, speaks of, calling it " unworthy communion." "He that eateth and drinketh unworthily, eateth and drinketh judgment to himself, not discerning the Lord's Body" (1 Cor. xi. 28).

To the evil disposed, who have no sincere disposition to continue always free from mortal sin, I would say: Take care how you receive. Turn about; change your hearts; cleanse your souls from sin before you presume to take the Lord's Body, that you may not eat and drink judgment or damnation to yourselves.

To the good girl, who lives habitually in the grace of God, I would say: You are already prepared. You could even go to Communion without confession; but I know very well you would not desire to do that, for even if it be not required to confess, you would wish to do it, and to be as well prepared as possible.

Make, then, with pure heart, confession of your faults, humbly desiring to amend them all, small as well as great. If any kind of cursing, be it ever so light, has fallen from your mouth, determine to stop it. If temper has overcome you sometimes, resolve to keep in mind the sweetness that Jesus desires of you ; to put down impatience, murmuring, and all such things. Determine to watch over and correct faults of neglect, wastefulness, and carelessness in performing your duty.

Make up your mind that truth, in all things, shall be told, and lying and deceitfulness be trodden under your feet, as unworthy one who receives the God of truth.

With such desires and such resolutions approach your confession, and you will make just the preparation the Holy Ghost puts in the mouth of King David : '' I will wash my hands in innocence, and so will I approach Thy altar, O my God '' (Ps. xxvi. 6). You will wash your heart with the Blood of Christ in holy Confession ; come out of it pure and innocent, and approach the altar, lovely in the eyes of the Lamb of God, Jesus, who loves above all things the whiteness of innocence, and purity from the stains of sin.

After Confession bear in mind that the time for your Communion is near, remember Who it is that is coming to visit you, and consider it the greatest and happiest event of your lives. Now is a good time to make acts of faith, contrition, love, humility, etc., either out of a book, or, if you can, out of your own hearts.

Promise, over and over again, to the Lord, that you will be for ever a most true and faithful servant of His, and that it shall be the study of your lives to observe such conduct and do such things as you think will be most pleasing to Him.

These generous resolutions will be most pleasing to Jesus, and as good a preparation as you could make. An entire offering of your whole heart and soul, mind and body, will and understanding, to be guided and governed by the holy will of Jesus Christ, made with your whole soul, will be the most acceptable offering you can make your Lord when you receive Him. This is enough to say about the preparation of the soul.

In respect to the body, you know you must be fasting from food and drink from midnight before the morning of your Communion. Should you have accidentally taken anything it is no sin, but you will have to put off your Communion until another day.

CHAPTER XXXVI.

BEHAVIOR AT AND AFTER COMMUNION.

GO to the altar neatly and modestly dressed out of respect to the Lord you are to receive; as the Scripture says, " Let your modesty be known unto all men " (Phil. iv. 5). Show piety and modesty in the way you approach and go away from the altar.

And take care to spend some time in devout prayers and thanksgiving after Communion. This is the very best time of all to pray, because Jesus is with you, on purpose to hear you. He is always present, it is true; for He is God, who is everywhere, but He gives us a peculiar claim to be heard and to get our requests when He comes to see us.

When a great person goes to see one in humble circumstances, he does not go with empty hands; so our Lord has abundance of graces to bestow on us when we ask for them after Communion.

The late Queen of Belgium, Maria Amelia, was a pious Christian; she thought more of following Jesus Christ's example than of all her royal splendor. So she used to slip out of her palace, dressed like a poor woman, with a large basket on her arm filled with warm clothing for the poor, with medicines and delicate food for the sick.

She would slip down into the cellars and under-ground rooms, where the poor people live, to comfort them and give them what they needed. And she smiled on them with so much affection, and spoke such kind words to them, that she made them forget all their poverty for a little while, in the sunshine of her presence.

This is what our Lord Jesus Christ does for us. He forgets who He is and comes into our hearts, poor and dark as they are, with nothing but sympathy· and kindness for us. The fact is, what the Queen of Belgium used to do was only a little spark which had kindled her heart out of that fire that burns all the time in the heart of Jesus Christ.

Spend then some time, at least fifteen minutes if you can, or half an hour, in talking with your Saviour and begging for all you need for body or soul, but especially for the soul, which is your great concern after all.

Sometimes we see people going to the altar to receive, and going out of church immediately after, without even waiting a short five minutes. I cannot help thinking in such cases of what happened once to our Saviour.

Ten men who had the leprosy came to Him and asked Him to heal them. He told them to go and show themselves to the priest, and as they started off to go they were all healed. But nine of them kept on, and only one turned back to give thanks to the Lord for His great kindness. "Oh!" said the Saviour, "ten were healed, but where are the nine? Only one has turned back to give thanks" (St. Luke xvii. 13, 14).

And after the thanksgiving is over, and you have gone home, from time to time during that day remember and cast a grateful look upon the Saviour for His goodness. St. Aloysius used to do this for a whole week after receiving. Oh, what benefits you will receive from such Communions!

Go, then, and receive regularly, and as often as your circumstances will permit.

CHAPTER XXXVII.

HOW OFTEN SHOULD ONE RECEIVE COMMUNION?

BUT how often should one receive Communion? That is for you to judge, with the advice of your confessor. As a general rule, for good girls who have the chance, I should say once a month would not be too often. It is the period chosen by most of those who are striving to lead devout lives, and experience shows that to communicate as often as that has the happiest effects on the soul. Most of our pious confraternities are established on the principle of monthly Communion, and the Church encourages the practice by many indulgences granted to them.

Besides, monthly Communion does not usually interfere too much with what one has to do.

Would that all our Catholic girls would take up this habit of Communion! I am sure a thousand evils that now exist among them would speedily be stopped. Some go more frequently, and if the heart burns for the love of God and with desire to receive the Saviour in Communion, there is no reason why it should not be gratified. Some of the saints received every day. The early Christians did so. As the Scripture says: "They continued in the daily breaking of bread"; by which is understood the Communion.

St. Catherine of Siena was one of those who were all on fire with the love of Jesus Christ, and she longed for Communion so much that finally she got permission to receive every day. This did not seem exactly right to a very worthy bishop, who perhaps did not understand how holy she was, and who was not accustomed to see people receive so often.

One day he said to her: " I am afraid you are not doing as you ought in receiving so often, for I remember what St. Augustine says about it: That to receive every day is a thing I neither praise nor blame, but to receive every Sunday I exhort you." She replied: " Well, Right Reverend Father, if St. Augustine does not blame me, why do you ?" He was so much struck by the force of this answer that he had no more to say.

But it is very few that, like these saints, can go every day. It is out of most people's power to go as often as that if they would. Indeed, very few can go as often as once a week, therefore I think once in the month suits for most people better than any other period.

I do not like once in the quarter, or more rarely, so well, but it may be that one cannot go oftener ; in such case God will take the will for the deed.

He looks at the heart, and if he sees in it an ardent desire to receive, though in fact we do not receive, for want of opportunity, he will not allow us to lose anything by it, but make it up to us abundantly in some other way.

So it was with the hermits of the desert, with St. Mary of Egypt and others who were far away from any priest, and who could receive only here and there at long intervals, when they had the opportunity, yet they are among the greatest of the saints.

To close the subject, let me relate to you how

St. Juliana received Holy Communion on her death-bed. Although of a noble family, she gave up all splendor and riches and chose for herself the portion of Jesus Christ, poverty and labor.

Her hard and severe life and continued abstinence brought on a weakness of the stomach, so that she was not able to retain the food she took, and on that account she could not receive Holy Communion.

Every one, however, noticed her wonderful patience and cheerfulness amid her distress. No complaint came from her mouth, except one. She found it hard to be deprived of the Blessed Sacrament. Her heart was fixed on Jesus her Saviour, and, amid her pains, could she only have received Him she would have been content.

She begged her confessor that as she could not receive, he would, at least, bring the Blessed Sacrament and place it on her breast. Her entreaties were so earnest that at last he yielded and complied with her request, but at the very moment he did so the Bread of Heaven disappeared, and Juliana, with serene and joyful countenance, breathed out her soul.

Those who were present could scarcely believe what they saw, until, when her chaste body was prepared for burial, the exact form of the sacred Host, bearing the image of Jesus crucified, was found stamped upon her left breast near the heart.

What an example of the desire of the devout soul to receive, and of the desire of Jesus to come to all those who long to receive Him!

CHAPTER XXXVIII.

ON SPECIAL DEVOTIONS.

" BUT please tell us, now that you have spoken of daily prayer and the Sacraments, what special devotions we ought to practise."

We read in the lives of the saints of their having different special devotions and reciting special prayers according to their devotion. For example, St. John Gualbert forgave the murderer of his brother, who begged forgiveness through the Five Sacred Wounds of our Lord, to which St. John had a special devotion.

St. Juliana had a special devotion to the Blessed Sacrament, and through her exertions the feast of Corpus Christi was established in honor of it.

Ven. Margaret Mary Alacoque was devoted to the Sacred Heart of our Lord, considering especially His love for us all.

St. Teresa speaks in the highest terms of devotion to St. Joseph, and of the benefits derived

from his intercession.   All the saints have had a
special devotion to our Blessed Lady.   Some of
them as the " Mother of Sorrows," some as the
" Refuge of Sinners," or the " Help of Christians," or to some particular mystery or event
of her life.

" What special devotion would you recommend to us?"   To answer this question we
must look into it a little.   What is the meaning
or idea of any special devotion whatever?   It is
nothing more nor less than a special or particular way of raising the soul to God, either by
viewing Him in a particular light, as, for example, in some circumstances of the life of our
Lord Jesus Christ, His Agony in the Garden,
His Five Wounds, or His Crucifixion, or as
present in the Blessed Sacrament, or the special
devotion to the Holy Ghost.   Or else in considering God's goodness and love and power as
shown in the life of the Blessed Virgin Mary, or
of the saints, and begging their prayers in our
behalf.

God must be the end of all our devotion.   To
learn to know Him and to love Him better, is
the sum and substance of all that we should propose to ourselves in all our prayers and all our
devotions.

All special devotions, of whatever kind they
may be, should be performed with the idea of
uniting ourselves more perfectly to God, and

not because others have performed them, or out of a mere routine or habit.

If they really nourish the soul and promote solid virtue, they may be practised; if they have not an effect of this kind, they are better let alone.

It appears to me that when a person is loaded down with a great number of special devotions and prayers, the soul is likely to be hindered rather than assisted in uniting itself to God by them.

And the reason of this is, that God Himself is not brought enough in view, but the mind rather taken up with such a number of things that it becomes either wearied out and distracted, or else we become merely creatures of a world of formal observances.

If a special devotion grows up naturally in our hearts, as, for example, when from reading the glorious actions of a particular saint we are powerfully excited to follow his example and pushed on to love God greatly, then it is very good, and we hope that saint will take an interest in us and beg his or her prayers. We love that saint and we set a great value on his love and assistance. We see from this how unfounded the idea is that special devotions lead us away from God, that they are in opposition to devotion to God. Why do we love to visit the good, listen to their conversation and beg their prayers? Because we are anxious to know and love God better, and these things help us on.

Devotion to the Blessed Virgin, or to St. Joseph, or an apostle or saint, is of precisely the same nature. We love and admire them because they are so much like God and so beloved by Him. We imitate them because their conduct was agreeable to God, and we beg their prayers because they are friends of God.

If devotion of a special nature is not produced by such a motive, it is good for nothing. If it takes the place of, and hinders the course of the soul to God, I am ready to admit that it is hurtful.

Suppose, for example, that a person should be running about begging the prayers of pious people without praying himself, we should not commend his conduct, although it is a good thing to ask the prayers of the pious.

So I am inclined to think that one who is occupied with a great round of litanies and special prayers to different saints, without thinking much of God, is on a false track of devotion.

But abuse of a thing or excess in it does not hinder the proper and discreet use of it, and special devotions to the Blessed Virgin and the saints are very profitable. Let us then refer them all to God, practise them all with a view to God's love, and the Holy Ghost will direct us when to use them, and how far each one of us may profitably carry them.

I will say something of devotion to the Blessed Sacrament, and to the Blessed Virgin Mary, and to the saints, all of which must find their place in a true life of devotion to God.

CHAPTER XXXIX.

OF DEVOTION TO THE BLESSED SACRAMENT.

WHEN the priest at the altar during the Mass pronounces the sacred words of consecration, that which was bread before ceases to be bread, and becomes the Body of Christ. He then raises this sacred Body, which is no less than Christ Himself, in his hands, above his head, the bell is rung, and all the faithful bow themselves down in humble adoration of their God and Saviour.

Under the appearance of bread is the Lord Jesus Christ, at whose very name "every knee shall bow of things in heaven, of things on the earth, and of things under the earth." And after the consecration Jesus remains in the sacred particle, or Host, as it is called, until it is consumed.

In the sacred Host within the Tabernacle is Jesus. There he remains night and day, and

as long as He is there He is entitled to be wor-
shipped and adored the same as when He was
raised on high during the Mass.

By devotion to the Blessed Sacrament I mean,
besides Mass and Communion, adoration, love,
and prayers to Jesus at other times, while He
remains on our altars.

As soon as we come into church what do we
see ? A light burning before the altar, to indicate the presence of God in the Sacrament. Not
God surrounded by thunder and lightning in
His majesty to judge us, but God in a humble,
silent form, to love us and do us good.

What an emotion of awe and veneration
should fill our souls when we think that God
Himself is present ! what love and gratitude
when we think how He is present, and why !
The Almighty God is present, but as one of us,
and our best friend.

Just as if we could see Jesus Christ sitting
there with a most gentle and benignant countenance, calling out to us and telling us to come
nearer and tell Him all about our affairs, what
weighs on our hearts and what we want Him
to do for us. Oh ! then, when we are in church,
do not let us forget for a moment who is there.
Do not let us be so disrespectful to the Lord as
to talk or laugh, but think of Him and pray to
Him.

"How dreadful is this place !" said Jacob,

when the Lord appeared to him; "this is no other but the house of God and the gate of heaven" (Gen. xxviii. 17). And Moses put off the shoes from his feet when the Lord showed Himself. "Take off thy shoes," said a voice to him, "for the place thou standest on is holy ground" (Ex. iii. 5).

Surely, when one has once been told of the presence of Christ in the Sacrament, I should think he could never, to the longest day of his life, forget himself so far as to indulge in the slightest light or unbecoming behavior.

You have heard how the magnet draws to itself pieces of iron; they fly to it and stick closely to it, because there is a power in that magnet which they cannot resist. So your hearts ought to be drawn to the tabernacle where Jesus is.

Oh! how I love to see the altar-rail surrounded with devout men and women praying. They get as close to Jesus as they can. How lively is their faith, and how strong their devout prayers, and how ardent their desires to be pleasing to Him! Then is the time grace is pouring into their souls.

After all, this is the great devotion of the Church. What can compare with it? You cannot be too devout to the Blessed Sacrament. When you get the opportunity, pay a visit to the Sacrament during the week.

If you had a very dear friend you would want to see that friend every day ; so desire to go and see the dearest and best Friend you have every day.

Go and nestle up as close as you can to that Friend who can protect you from all harm and fill you with consolation.

If you cannot actually make the visit to the church, make one in spirit by turning towards the place where the Sacrament is kept and devoutly lifting up your soul to Him.

If the priest should happen at any time to open the tabernacle when you are in church, kneel at once in adoration of the Saviour exposed to view.

If the Sacrament is brought to any house where you are, take care that everything shall be prepared beforehand : the room swept and put in order, a table with a clean white cloth, a crucifix, and a lighted candle upon it.

In all things and in all places show that you know well the honor and respect due to your Lord and Saviour.

Another devotion most agreeable to God and useful to yourself is what is called spiritual communion ; that is, to excite a longing desire in your heart of receiving Communion, and to love the Lord and to pray to Him the same as if you had actually received.

Many holy persons have found great comfort

and help from this practice. Blessed Joanna of the Cross declared she received the same graces from her spiritual as from her actual communion. "O excellent method of communicating!" she exclaimed, "in which one does not need to make confession, nor ask permission, nor the help of any but God alone."

How beautiful to be able as often as one likes to draw near to Jesus and receive Him in spirit, with a lively faith, almost as one would at the altar itself. Many souls will find a great help in such kind of devotions.

CHAPTER XL.

ON DEVOTION TO THE BLESSED VIRGIN MARY.

NEXT to devotion to the Blessed Sacrament, which is beyond comparison above and before all others, as God is above all creatures, comes the devotion to the Blessed Virgin Mary, the Mother of our Divine Saviour.

Why should we cherish a tender love for her? Because she is the mother of our Lord. How can we love the Lord without loving her, who is His own mother? How foolish it is then to try to separate the love of the one from that of the other, or the devotion of the one from that of the other!

All true love and true devotion to the Blessed Virgin is grounded on our love for our Lord Jesus Christ. She took care of Him, she is the most beloved by Him, she was the most worthy to be His mother, and she is His mother.

Of course, then, she is above all the saints, and deserves especial love and veneration. And she has always had it, and always will have it, according to her own prophecy : '' Behold, from henceforth all nations shall call me blessed '' (St. Luke i. 48).

And as the Blessed Virgin is nearest and dearest to Jesus Christ, so is her power to help us greatest. How can the Saviour refuse anything to His own mother? If we desire anything from Him, we cannot do better than to add to our own prayers those of His mother, and beg her to intercede for us.

Pray earnestly and frequently to the mother of God : expose all your wants to her, and that you may be agreeable to her cherish a deep and tender love to her. And what kind of love is most suitable? That of a child to the best of mothers.

When St. Teresa lost her mother her heart was breaking with grief. She was very young at the time, and in the simplicity of her heart she knelt down and said to the Blessed Virgin : '' Now my mother is dead, I have no one to take care of me ; you must be a mother to me as long as I live," shedding a torrent of tears at the same time. What a good mother the Blessed Virgin proved herself to St. Teresa; and what a consoling thought it is that a poor girl amid all her temptations, severe trials and afflictions, can have the blessed thought of that dear mother in Heaven watching over her with loving eyes, and with all a mother's interest, in her truest welfare. That surely is enough to make a gleam of sunshine in the darkest day for the soul.

But if we would have this good mother for our own, we must take care to make ourselves agreeable to her. And how is that best done? I will tell you. Love her Son dearly, and she will love you dearly. And how shall her Son be loved dearly? By following his own example that he set us while he lived upon earth. By following the pure, the humble, innocent, charitable, example his own mother the Virgin herself has set us.

Ask yourself frequently, How would Jesus Christ, how would the Blessed Virgin, act under these circumstances? how would they be pleased to see me act? and then act accordingly. "Learn of me," says our Lord, "for I am meek and humble of heart." Of what use is it to recite devotions, to say the Rosary, or wear the Scapular, when you pay no attention to imitate the conduct of the Blessed Virgin?

Some wear the Scapular and lead wicked lives. They say: "One cannot be eternally lost who wears the Scapular." Now, one who encourages himself to go on in wickedness with the idea of being preserved from the consequences of sin by wearing the Scapular, instead of getting any good from it, will only be making his damnation more certain.

The Scapular was intended as a badge of the true, faithful servants of Mary, who strive to live lives worthy of such a badge and of such an example. Great graces are annexed to wearing it with such an intention, but none to a superstitious and wicked use of it, such as I have described above.

A true soldier honors his uniform by his conduct. He stands to his colors as to his life, and so those who wear the Scapular should remember that they must walk worthy of that blessed habit and uniform of the Blessed Virgin with which they have been invested. We may think that a person of this sort, who wears the Scapular, cannot be lost, but not so of any other.

Living, then, in such a way as to please the Mother of God, we may invoke her assistance with great confidence in all our temptations, for she is able and willing to help us. Particularly is this the case in those against the virtue of purity. This most pure Virgin seems peculiarly ready to help us to keep that virtue which was so peculiarly her own. In all temptations, at the very first thought, fly to her protection. Pronounce the holy names of Jesus and Mary, and you will be strengthened so that you will not give the least consent to such a horrid temptation.

Pray a good deal to the Holy Virgin, either out of books, reciting her litany, Little Office, or other prayers; or use that excellent devotion, the Rosary; or pray out of the heart, talking familiarly and lovingly with her, and thinking over her life, and how yours may be like it.

Devotion to our Lady will make you understand better what the Lord has done for you in becoming a little child, and having a real woman for his mother, and deepen your love for Him. So that the Church rightly considers this true devotion to the Mother of God of very great consequence in reference to the love of God, which is the aim and end of our existence here in this world.

CHAPTER XLI.

DEVOTION TO SAINTS.

PRAY to the saints. They stand in the presence of God, and are His dear friends. They have gone through what we will have to go through. They know well our dangers and our trials. Let us pray for their intercession, and they will pray for us.

Let us imitate their virtues, their humility, patience, meekness, charity, etc. What flesh and blood, by the grace of God, has done, can be done again by the same grace. To think of the saints and examine their lives is a wonderful encouragement to us.

I cannot understand why those outside of the Church should entertain so much repugnance to the doctrine of the intercession of the saints. It seems to be the very first and foremost of all their objections to our Holy Faith, that we pray to the Blessed Virgin and the saints, and yet nothing is more natural and more in accordance with reason and religion, or more consoling and encouraging.

How often we hear such expressions as these: "You Catholics are idolatrous; you pray to the saints. You Catholics place the

Virgin Mary and the saints in place of God; in place of the Saviour. Do you not pray to them?" "Yes." "Well, then, what need is there of further proof? You confess all that we have accused you of." Not at all; we pray to the saints, but it by no means follows that we put them in any way in place of God or of our Saviour.

If it did follow, then it must equally follow that we are guilty of idolatry if we ask a friend or pious acquaintance to pray for us. We put that friend or acquaintance just as much in the place of the Saviour, when we ask his prayers, as we do the saint when we ask his prayer. Every prayer to the Blessed Virgin or the saints is a prayer for their help, or for their prayers with God, or what is called "interces-sion"; there is nothing about it, in any way that goes beyond the help or intercession of a friend in this world.

"But how do we know they can hear our prayers? Is not that making them equal to God, to suppose them to know everything that goes on in the world, in all its different parts at the same time?"

No, it is not. I know a vast number of things that go on all over the world, a short time after they happen, by looking into the newspaper of a morning; but I know very little after all; and if a saint, whose soul is with

God, in His very presence, should look into God's all-knowledge, and see there, as in a mirror, all that is going on in the world, that he cares to know or is interested about, or all about the salvation of all the souls struggling in the world, it would not be much, after all, compared with the infinite wisdom of God. People who make such objections ought to think a little bit on God's infinite wisdom, and they will answer their own objections without troubling any one else with them.

The Scripture tells us we are encompassed with a cloud of witnesses. "And therefore we also having so great a cloud of witnesses over us, laying aside every weight and the sin that surroundeth us, by patience let us run to the fight proposed to us" (Hebrews xii. 1).

Who are those "witnesses over us"? Abraham and Isaac and Jacob, Joseph and Moses, and all those who in old times lived by faith in God's fear, and are now dead. These, as well as the prophet Jeremias, are they who are "Lovers of their brethren and of the people of Israel," and "who pray much for the people and for all the holy city" (2 Macc. xv. 14).

And, indeed, our own hearts tell us how proper and right it is that our friends in the other world should know and feel in regard to all that interests our eternal salvation. We rejoice in the thought that a mother, or sister, or brother is watching over us from the heaven of happiness, and helping us in our troubles.

I have heard it myself from the lips of Protestant ministers, in their prayers at funerals, and all the bystanders approved of it, although it was nothing more nor less than the Catholic doctrine of the intercession of saints which these same people are so shocked at in the practice of the Catholic Church.

Think over the example of the saints, particularly of those which instruct you the most and excite you most strongly to the love and service of God. Thus you will keep up the "communion of saints," and draw down upon yourselves many blessings.

CHAPTER XLII.

TRUE IDEA OF SERVICE.

NOW, my dear girls, if there be any grumblers among you, I am not going to leave you a single word to say. I don't care how many complaints you have to make, or what troubles you have to endure. If you are under the most disagreeable and hardest foreman in the factory, or have the crossest old woman for a mistress that ever lived, or ever so hard work to do, or low wages, or poor fare, and no thanks, I don't care : I am determined to make you own up that it is all first-rate, and could not be better.

I am going to shut your mouths. And how shall I go to work to do it, particularly as there are some whose mouths it is not easy to shut? In the same way that they shut up a child's mouth : by putting a big sugar-plum in it. I am going to show you the sweetest and most heart-cheering words, spoken by the Holy Ghost, about your service : words which ought to make the tears start to your eyes when you read them, and your hearts leap with joy.

Listen to these words : '' Servants, obey in all things your masters according to the flesh, not serving to the eye as pleasing men, but in simplicity of heart, fearing God. Whatsoever you do, do it from the heart, as to the Lord and not to men '' (Col. iii. 22).

Understand well the meaning of these words. All your service is here taken by the Lord as if it were His own service. How happy you must think those holy women were who went around with our Lord Jesus Christ, ministering to His wants, and following Him wherever He went, to prepare His food and lodging ; but you see by these words that you can do the same thing for our Lord Jesus Christ, if in simplicity of heart and a pure intention you weave cloth in the factory, stand behind the counter to sell goods, do any other kind of work for your employer, or do the cooking and make the beds for the family in which you live.

In the last day, if you do your duties with this spirit of doing all for the Lord and not for men, the Lord will say to you: "Come, ye blessed of My Father, possess the kingdom prepared for you from the foundation of the world. For I was hungry, and ye gave me to eat: I was thirsty, and ye gave me to drink," etc. (St. Matt. xxv. 35). Then you will say: "Lord, when did we ever see Thee hungry and feed Thee, thirsty and give Thee drink?" and the Lord shall reply: "Did I not tell you to perform all your duties in simplicity of heart as to Me, and not as to men? You have done so, and I reckon it all as done to Myself."

When the work comes hard, and you are tired out standing all day at the loom or running your sewing-machine, or scrubbing the floors, or washing the clothes or the dishes, think, "I am doing all this for my Lord Jesus Christ." Not a single drop of sweat, not a single pain or ache is without his notice. Do such work with cheerfulness, as being glad to suffer something in Christ's service, and all your heartache, at least, will disappear. You will be wonderfully sustained and supported, no matter what may be your trial.

The Lord Jesus Christ knew well that a poor

girl who has to earn her living would have a
good deal to suffer, and a good deal to put up
with.   His heart was filled with compassion,
and He determined to raise her condition so
high as to be above and beyond all its sorrows
and miseries, just as a high mountain in the
clear blue air is above all the smoke and filthy
fogs of the low swamps.

How has He done this?   By raising her service to the dignity and greatness of a service
done to Himself.   Kings and queens cannot be
more than servants of the Most High.   You,
then, are raised to the level of kings and queens
and more, for the Lord has never so lovingly
promised to accept their service as He has yours.

CHAPTER XLIII.

TRUE   IDEA   OF   SERVICE.—HOW   TO   CORRE-
SPOND   TO   IT.

BUT in order to gain all the advantage the
Lord offers you, you must bear in mind the
conditions he requires of you: "Servants, be
obedient in all things to your masters, not serving to the eye as pleasing men, but in simplicity
of heart, fearing God.   Whatsoever you do, do
it from the heart, as to the Lord, and not to
men."

That means, Do your duty, and do it well. Do it as well as if you saw the Lord looking at you, and were doing it for Him. Do not at all consider who your employer may be, but look at Christ.

If the mistress is ill-favored and ill-tempered, or handsome and gracious, let it be all one to you. Our Blessed Saviour is beautiful and gracious enough, and, after all, it is He whom you are serving.

Suppose the mistress is overbearing and hard to please—it's "Bridget, here" and "Bridget, there," without rhyme or reason; never mind—every time you go here or go there the Lord is pleased and delighted with your ready and cheerful obedience to that overbearing and difficult mistress.

Suppose your mistress is fussy, and thinks she knows a good deal more than she does know, and wants to have her own way, when your way is better; let her have her own way; obey readily and pleasantly; that is the way to please the Lord.

Suppose she scolds you unjustly, when you have committed no fault; bear it patiently: let the storm blow over. For it is the Lord that has placed her over you, and who says, "Obey in all things"—that is to say, where there is no sin or wrong.

And this is true whatever may be your employment, whether in the shop or in the factory, or if you do work at home for others, endeavor to be as faithful and as willing as if you were working for our Lord Himself.

If you think there is just cause of complaint, or you could better your condition elsewhere, you are at liberty to leave; but as long as you are there observe this line of conduct, and your service will be all for the Lord.

You know how it is when you look out of the window at a pleasant prospect; you do not stop to consider the glass you look through. So do not stop to consider the faults or imperfections of your employers; see only Jesus, your Master and your best Friend, shining through them. If you live with a Jew, or a heathen even, that makes no difference; only consider that they represent the Lord to you. Try in every way to show obedience, respect, and duty to them.

If a little, dirty, impudent girl were to bring a message to you from your mistress, you would not consider who brings it, but who sends it, and you would obey it. So think—no matter who your employers may be—that all their commands have been sent by the Lord to you, through their means, and that you are fulfilling them for Him. That is the way the saints looked at things, and they delighted in nothing so much as to do that kind of work which others despised.

CHAPTER XLIV.

TRUE IDEA OF SERVICE.—EXAMPLES.

ST. AMEDÉE, who was of a noble family, a relative of the Emperor Conrad, begged permission to clean the shoes of his brethren, and rub them over with stinking grease. One day his uncle, a nobleman, came to see him, and found him greasing these old, dirty, rough shoes. Do you think he was scandalized at the sight? Not a bit. He thanked God that his nephew understood so well the blessing and the nobility of being a servant of Jesus Christ.

In the good old Catholic times, when faith was warm, masters and mistresses understood so well the advantages of serving others, that they themselves used sometimes to become servants, and wait upon their own servants and serve the poor.

St. Harvia, the wife of the Duke of Silesia, used to be taken sometimes for a servant, while she was feeding and waiting upon more than fifty poor persons in the great hall of her husband's castle.

How different is this conduct from that of many a girl, who, when she is sometimes called upon for a service a little out of her line, and especially if she considers it a little lower than her ordinary work, says: "I'm not going to black shoes for anybody," "I'm nobody's nigger." And that, too, when she knows it is right to call on her under the circumstances, and that she ought to do it without a word. Such a one forgets all about serving the Lord.

I remember well a lady, who was not above sweeping out the church of God herself, mildly asking a Catholic girl to help her, and what did she get for an answer? "I'm nobody's nigger!" You see this girl was not willing to be a servant of Christ, even in His own house. O Pride! what do you not lead people to do?

Of St. Mary Magdalen of Pazzi it is said: "She regarded God in all whom she served, and taught her sisters to do the same, saying: 'You should think yourselves unworthy to serve souls, who are the tabernacles of the Holy Ghost, and see God in all.' Although she was a choir-sister, and not obliged to work with the lay-sisters, she chose to do it. Nothing pleased her better than to make the bread, scour out the pots and kettles, and do the heavy washing. She would rise in the night, before a soul was stirring in the house, make the fire, draw the water, and put on the clothes to boil. She used sometimes to send around and gather up all the dirty clothes in the day-time, and go down and wash them all out at night. Whenever others were working with her she took on herself the hardest of the work, and would insist on doing it all herself, if they would let her. She would say : ' Now I know you are tired, go and rest, and let me do it.' ''

Yet she was a lady by birth and education, and had everything in her father's house that heart could wish. Why did she do all this? Simply because she considered Christ in all she did. In the simplicity of her heart she did it as if it were all done for the Lord.

St. Vincent of Paul was obliged to enter the service of Mr. De Gondi, to educate his children. Now listen to the way in which he discharged his duties : '' To sanctify himself in this new office, he proposed to himself to honor Jesus Christ in the person of Mr. De Gondi, the Blessed Virgin in that of his wife, and the disciples of our Saviour in those of the servants of the family.

'' He candidly acknowledged that this manner of acting, which seemed extremely simple, was of great service to him; and that seeing God alone, under different aspects, in all the persons with whom he was engaged, obliged him to do nothing before men which he would not have done before our Lord Jesus Christ, if he had had the happiness of seeing Him and talking with Him when He was on the earth '' (*Life of St. Vincent of Paul*).

Now, girls, I would like to ask if I have not been as good as my word, and shut the mouths of all the grumblers and complainers? Have I not shut up their mouths with the sweetest sugar-plum?

In all your hard work, all scoldings and fault-findings, in all that touches your pride or your feelings, have I not put you right in the presence of Jesus Christ, who whispers in your ears: "Never mind, my good girl; it is not for Mrs. Smith, nor Mrs. Jones, nor Mrs. Anybody-else you have to do this; it is for Me, your Saviour, who loves you dearly. The time is soon coming when you will be amply rewarded for it all. Do it patiently, do it humbly, do it without repining—in one word, with a good will, and I accept all as done to Myself."

Now, to sum up all that has been said in answer to the question: In what spirit should you discharge your duties? I say: Look neither to the right nor to the left, but look at Jesus Christ above, and do all for Him, and as you think will best please Him.

CHAPTER XLV

MANY a Catholic girl has been good at home, has attended to her duties, and to all appearances has loved her religion, and yet after a little while at service all her piety seems to have disappeared.

She does not go to Mass, she goes gadding about the streets day and night, talks all kind of talk, spends her wages foolishly, and becomes what you may call a wicked girl; at least she is anything but in the grace of God.

A good deal of this has been brought about by her getting into an unsuitable place, where bad companions or evil example has destroyed her good principles.

A really good girl, who strives to obey the voice of God in her heart—that is, her conscience —will, I feel sure, sooner or later get a good place, for she is worth her weight in gold to her employer. But she may, at first, have to take up with places that are not very good, until her true merit is found out. She ought, however, to be on the lookout to find a place suitable to her ; and what kind of place is that?

I can only give some general directions, and

then leave the rest to each one's prudence and good sense. You should try to get some kind of employment in which you will be favorably situated for leading a virtuous and holy life. That is, certainly, the very first thing to be attended to.

Some, and it may be not bad-intentioned, girls are so carried away with the idea of high wages that they think of nothing else. A dollar or a half a dollar more a month carries the day with them, although they run the risk of losing what money cannot buy—that is, purity and innocence of soul.

Girls in good places, where they have every privilege of attending Mass, where they have time and fine opportunities for prayer, where they have a quiet, respectable home, get their heads turned on hearing that they can get a trifle more wages somewhere else. Nothing will do but they must go there, and they find out that they cannot get to Mass at all, or very seldom ; that the work is harder, and that they are kept in a state of confusion the whole time, so that they can scarcely pray at all.

Now, surely, there is no objection to a girl's trying to get good wages. If she can get the highest wages going, I do not blame her. She has to get her living, and has good uses for all she can earn. I do not blame her for desiring not to be overworked, and to have a comfortable situation.

But these things are not the first of all to be looked out for. We should attend to spiritual advantages first, and then we may look to other things. "Seek first the kingdom of God and His justice, and other things shall be added to you" (St. Matt. vi. 33).

I would advise you then, in the first place, to avoid, if possible, engaging yourselves in hotels, taverns, inns, saloons, or other places where there is a crowd of people, and where gambling or drinking is carried on. In such places there are generally a number of persons employed at service. Now, you know the old saying, that one scabby sheep infects the whole flock, so when there are many working together some are almost sure to be bad, and to exercise a bad influence on the good. Besides, I know very well that a great deal of sin of different kinds is apt to be carried on in such places, which makes them unfit for a modest, pious young woman.

Who would like to live with a number of others, be obliged to eat at the same table, talk with them, and see them constantly, when some of them are neglecters of all their religious duties; others filthy in their conversation; others full of bad temper and spitefulness; others full of little petty dishonesty, and neglecting their duties in the house ?

What kind of a place is it for a good girl

where drinking and carousing, cursing and swearing, and filthy talk is going on all around? Go to no place whatever where you can foresee that you will be obliged to live in the midst of open and unblushing sin, but where there is at least decency, and a chance to take care of yourself in quiet.

To be sure, there are hotels which are respectable enough, and I do not doubt that a good girl might possibly live a good life in them. I have known very good women in such places; but, after all, even the best are poor places for most young women; a private family is much more suitable.

Among private families, no doubt such as are Catholic are to be preferred to others, provided they are good and practical. As to careless and indifferent Catholic families, I have not a word to say in their favor; indeed, among them the temptation to become careless and indifferent may be greater than among Protestants.

And after all, most girls who live out must find situations among those who are not Catholic, because the number of Catholic families is small compared with the rest.

Now, among Protestant families, which should a good girl prefer? Those in which she is at liberty to attend her religious duties. She should always inquire before she engages herself: " How often can I be allowed to attend Mass?" Unless what might be called a reasonable answer, under the circumstances, is given to this question, I should certainly go further and try for something more satisfactory.

Also there should be nothing required that will hinder entire freedom of conscience. No employer, who is likely to be a good one, will ever think of interfering with your religious rights. The same freedom of conscience which they claim for themselves they will be ready to allow to others.

Do not engage anywhere where attendance at family prayers is required, for it is unjust for them to demand it and improper for you to comply. Say to all such, " I say my own prayers, and will try to discharge my duties faithfully ; more than that I cannot and will not do." If this is not satisfactory, go somewhere else.

If it is all right in regard to your religious duties, inquire into other circumstances ; see whether the duties are such as you are able to discharge, for you have no right to undertake what you cannot perform. Find out how many are in the family, and how many other persons are employed. See them if you can, and judge whether on the whole you can live with them to advantage.

There are many things which a prudent girl

can judge of better by her own eyes and ears than by what any one can tell her. Let her, then, with prayer to God, go about this business of choosing a place with a good motive to start on, and all the prudence she is possessed of, and do the best she can, with resignation to the divine will. God will be sure to place her, not perhaps where it is in all respects the most pleasant and agreeable to nature, but where it is most profitable and best for her.

CHAPTER XLVI.

HOW TO REGARD ONE'S EMPLOYERS.

WHERE both parties to the agreement are good Catholics, filled heart and soul with a desire to do the will of God, and working out their salvation with all the earnestness it deserves, the relation between them becomes a most beautiful one.

The workman endeavors to please his employer, doing all that has to be done, not because he is compelled to do it, but of a good will, remembering the Scripture : "With a good will doing service, as unto the Lord and not to men, knowing that whatsoever good every one shall do the same he shall receive of the Lord, whether bond or free " (Eph. vi. 7).

He obeys his employer in the simplicity of his heart, as he would obey Jesus Christ—that is, with the utmost respect and affection. Such a one will say to himself: " We are brothers in Jesus Christ, both redeemed by His precious blood, both equal in all Christian privileges, both equal in God's sight, with whom there is no respect of persons ; and which of us shall be highest in heaven will depend on who has been the most faithful in our station on earth. But I must remember that we have been placed by God's will in different positions. My dignity and honor, in God's sight, will depend on my not forgetting for a moment the position He has placed me in, and in behaving accordingly.

Such a one will not feel degraded or lowered one bit by obeying any just demands. He will feel a noble pride and honor in performing them. No matter what it is he has to do, whether it is cleaning out sewers, or feeding pigs, or blacking boots, or washing dirty clothes ; it makes no difference. All these things are quite indifferent in themselves, and when it comes in the line of duty to do them, it is a glory and honor for us to do them.

Take a doctor, for example ; let him come to visit his sick patient ; suppose he wears a gold watch and has on white kid gloves, he must dress loathsome sores, and he must perform oftentimes the most disagreeable offices, and if he does not do it, it is a shame and disgrace to him, both in the eyes of God and of men.

So, a good Catholic will throw overboard all foolish and hateful pride, and accept from the heart his position and all that it brings along with it, and simply look to do its duties, cheerfully, to the best of his power. He will love his employer at the same time that he serves him. His employer's interest will be his own. The children of the family will be dear to him ; in short, the house will be truly his home, and his employers will be like second father and mother to him.

And the good employer will entertain corresponding sentiments towards his dependents. He will remember the words of the Holy Ghost, who, after telling those who serve what their conduct ought to be, says : " And you, masters, do the same thing to them, forbearing threatenings ; knowing that the Lord both of them and you is in heaven, and there is no respect of persons with Him " (Eph. vi. 9).

Such a master will never forget that all in his employ are his brethren in Jesus Christ, and he will feel a deep interest in their welfare, both of soul and body.

A good mistress will be anxious that her domestics should attend Mass every Sunday, and regulate the household accordingly. She will endeavor to have them attend to Confession and

Communion ; warn them against extravagance, light behavior, and bad company. We have an example of this in the Prince de Condé, who would have his servants attend Mass every day. He used to notice even if the smallest boy was absent, and watched over their conduct as if he felt a responsibility for their souls.

To a good man his dependents will be in many respects like his own children. Of course, then, he will " forbear threatenings," that is, harsh conduct, when it is uncalled for. Children must be threatened sometimes for their own good, so must those who work carelessly, but it will not be done in an unfeeling and domineering way. He will never look down upon and despise those under him, but respect them as brethren in the Lord. And for one who has served him faithfully he will feel the deepest respect as well as affection.

CHAPTER XLVII.

CONTINUATION.—EXAMPLES.

HOW beautifully this mutual confidence and love is described in the Bible in the case of Abraham and his oldest servant, Eliezer, whom he had set over all his goods. Abraham trusted him with everything, even to go and choose a wife for his son Isaac. He explained to him all his wishes, and made him take an oath that he would not pick out a wife for his son among the heathen women of the Chanaanites, but go to the country and kindred from whence he had come and get one.

Now listen to the conduct of this good servant: When he came to the town where the kindred of Abraham dwelt, he made this prayer; "O Lord, the God of my master Abraham, meet me to-day, I beseech thee, and show kindness to my master Abraham" (Gen. xxiv. 12).

What a love and veneration, what an interest in all that concerned his master, is shown in these words! And when he had succeeded, by God's help, in discharging the duty which he was sent upon, he was as thankful as if it had been his own matter, and he says: "Falling down I adored the Lord, blessing the Lord God of my master Abraham, who hath brought me the straight way to take the daughter of my master's brother for his son" (Gen. xxiv. 48).

The good old man forgets himself in the affection he bears to Abraham and his son Isaac. There is no false pride here, he is not a bit ashamed to speak all the time of his master Abraham. He never overstepped the limit of perfect respect, and yet I am sure there was so much fidelity and goodness about him that he had pretty much his own way, being ruler, as the Scripture says, over all that Abraham had.

Where such feelings exist between both parties, we find them living together for years; for such employers would feel the loss of a faithful helper almost as the loss of a child, and the feeling is the same on the other side.

" What a charm," says the Baron de Prelle, "when masters and servants grow old together! What a joy to old age when it is served by ancient domestics, accustomed to its mode of life! I have known no house happier in this respect than that of the great Séguier, Chancellor of France. All his servants had grown old with him, and if we did not always see the same faces, we saw always the same persons. As their constitutions were not so strong as his own most of them broke down on the way, and he saw them die before himself, leaving but little behind them, though after forty years' service in the house of a chancellor."

So it is written of the great empress, the mother of Charles the Sixth, that at her death she assembled all her household and took leave of them, even to the lowest little servant, calling them by name.

Of the lovely little St. Zita, we read that, her parents hearing of a pious family among the nobility with whom they felt sure their daughter would have a good chance to live virtuously, they brought her to them at the age of twelve years.

At first, before her goodness became known, she was scolded a good deal, and spoken harshly to ; but she accepted all so humbly that after a little while they loved her dearly, and even held her in great veneration. There she lived, without ever changing her place, for nearly fifty years, until she was carried to her grave. She loved the children dearly and they loved her. She was always delighted to do them any kindness. It is said in her Life that she felt like a mother to them, and was always ready to take the nurse's place and relieve her of fatigue and annoyance.

Such ought to be the relation between employers and domestics, where both are Catholics. But, alas! that there are so many cases in which good Catholics are despised or disliked by their domestics. Sometimes the very reason why a girl is dissatisfied and seeks another place is, because a real interest is felt in having her well cared for in all respects, and in seeing her live a good life.

" I declare, there is no living in this house, where you can't do anything without being brought up for it ! What business is it to the madam whether I go to Mass or not ? I wish she'd let me alone. I declare, I never will live in a Catholic family again ; I'll go among Protestants, where I sha'n't always be bothered about going to church and going to confession, and keeping fast days, and keeping abstinence, and this and that. I wish folks would mind their own business !" Such is the language of many a girl who calls herself a Catholic, but who shows little of the spirit of one.

Another good girl has a first-rate Catholic home, where she is liked, and where she gets the highest wages, and light work, and every privilege, and where she might live as long as she likes. All goes along as well as possible for awhile. Then she gets restless. She must have a change ; some little foolish annoyance perhaps works on her mind, or, more likely, a mere fancy. She must change her place.

She gets a notion to go with somebody to California, as waiting-maid or cook ; or to Australia, or somewhere or other. Off she goes in spite of everything, and in a month's time she would almost give her right hand to be back again.

At other times she will go off to a Protestant family, where she gets less wages, has harder work, cannot get out to Mass, or to see her friends, and all merely out of a light, foolish head, that does not seem to have a grain of good sense in it. This restlessness is, I have no doubt, a kind of sickness, like home-sickness; and the only way to treat it is, to despise it; to pray to God, and seek peace in your heart in Him in whom alone you can find it. If you change your place on account of it, you only make it worse.

You know how a kernel of corn on a hot griddle flies about, jumps here and jumps there, and can't be still a minute, when it once gets going. So it will be with you, if you are weak enough to go away from a good place for such frivolous and light reasons.

Put up with a great deal of real difficulty, when you have got a good place, before you think of leaving it. If another girl there is bad, and therefore is disagreeable to you, wait awhile; she may be sent off or go away.

Remember the proverb: "A rolling stone gathers no moss"; and the other: "Go farther and fare worse." Many a girl has found it so, to her own sorrow. No employer is absolutely perfect and faultless, any more than you are yourself. Don't fly in a passion, then, when anything disagreeable happens. If they are really good in the main, put up with a defect or fault in them now and then. Overlook it; it will all come right in a little while. They have, no doubt, as much to put up with from you as you from them.

If St. Zita had flown into a passion when she was scolded unjustly, she would have lost the best of places and the happiest life in the world, and never, never, would have become a saint and honored over the whole world, as she is now.

CHAPTER XLVIII.

CONTINUATION.

BUT you may say to me : " It is seldom or never that these most delightful relations can exist nowadays. There are few who are bound together by the ties of the same faith, and who are actuated by such pure and holy motives in their conduct.

" The employers are, for the most part, Protestant, and many of them very indifferent in principle, and very difficult to get along with." Well, now, let us look into it a little.

Suppose you are in what you might call a good place, among those who are not Catholics. They respect your religion enough to let you alone about it, and afford you all reasonable privileges in exercising it. In regard to other things they are kind, and feel an interest in you. What is to hinder love and affection towards them? They certainly in such case deserve it.

I know many instances where such employers would do anything almost for the welfare of a good girl living with them. Mutual respect and affection can exist here in a high degree. I do not say that it will be as great as if they were of the household of faith: that cannot be expected; but nothing hinders it from being very great. Nothing hinders one from living happily and contentedly in such a place all one's life.

But suppose you live with a very fashionable lady who takes little interest in her domestics. Suppose she has not the way about her to be on pleasant terms with those of her household, yet is satisfied if things go along right, sometimes speaks a word or so, but does not seem to give herself much trouble about it anyway.

Of course, you could not be expected to be so much attached to her, in such a case. But you can mind your own affairs, and take what good words you get in a good spirit; think well of her as far as possible, and thank God that you have after all a good home where you can serve Him.

But now we can suppose something else. The mistress is cross and peevish, and finds fault when she has no right to. Her temper often occasions a good deal of heart-burning. Many of her ways are excessively disagreeable.

Still you must remember, in that case, the authority she has from God Himself; she is set over you while you are in her house, and as you would not be justified in abusing your father or mother, even if they were ill-tempered, so you are not justified in railing against her.

To sum up all, you should endeavor to show your employers respect in all cases; to feel as much interest as you can, as a member of the family; and as much affection and love as is possible, considering their character and conduct.

CHAPTER XLIX.

DOCTRINE OF SCRIPTURE ON THIS SUBJECT.

THE Holy Scripture clearly lays down this doctrine : " Let servants be subject to their masters, pleasing them in all things, not contradicting, not defrauding, but in all things showing good fidelity, that they may adorn the doctrine of God our Saviour in all things " (Titus ii. 9).

What does the Holy Ghost say to those persons who work for Catholics? Pay particular attention to the words, for they are full of meaning : " But they who have believing masters, let them not despise them because they are brethren, but serve them rather, because they are faithful and beloved " (1 Tim. vi. 2).

This seems to be very strange advice to give —to tell a man not to despise his master because he is good and amiable towards him. What can be the meaning of it?

I will tell you. The good, kind employer puts aside all pride and haughtiness, and speaks kindly and with some degree of familiarity to all his dependents. Now, when the person spoken to is proud, with but little good sense, he takes this all wrong.

He loses respect, and begins to get impudent and disagreeable. The Holy Ghost means to warn us against such conduct, and says what amounts to this : If your employers, in wishing to make you happy, and out of Christian love and interest in you, treat you as a friend and a child, do not take advantage of such treatment to be impudent and disagreeable to them.

Do not let the devil fill your heart with wicked pride, to despise them and disobey them; but rather be more anxious to serve them with faithfulness and love.

The same remark applies to every kind and loving employer, whether he belong to the "household of faith " or not, and whatever the employment may be. There is the same temptation to forget one's self through pride, and the same obligation to be more humble, respectful, and attentive.

Now, what is said of unreasonable and ill-tempered employers ? " Servants, be subject to your masters with all fear ; not only to the good and gentle, but also to the froward'' (1 Peter ii. 15)—*i.e.*, to the cross and ill-tempered. " For this is worthy of thanks, if for conscience towards God a man endure sorrows, suffering wrongfully. For what glory is it, if, sinning and being buffeted, you suffer it? But if, doing well, you suffer patiently, this is thank-worthy before God '' (1 Peter ii. 19, 20).

And the example of our Saviour is given to add weight to this : "For unto this you have been called ; because Christ also suffered for us, leaving you an example that you should follow His steps. Who did no sin, neither was guile found in His mouth. Who, when He was reviled did not revile : when He suffered, He threatened not, but delivered Himself to him that judged Him unjustly " (1 Peter ii. 22, 23).

CHAPTER L.

OF DILIGENCE.

THE great Apostle, St. Paul, when he stood before King Agrippa, gave an account of his conversion and labors. He says that at midday a great light from heaven shone around him exceeding the brightness of the sun, which struck himself and his companions to the ground, and that a voice spoke to him, telling him that he was chosen to open the eyes of the people who were in darkness, and to bring them to enjoy the lot of the saints in heaven.

Now he adds: "I was obedient to the heavenly vision, preaching everywhere to the Jews and the gentiles" (Acts xxvi. 19, 20). We all know how he labored with his whole heart and soul, suffering pains, afflictions, fatigues, persecutions, almost passing belief, until he closed his eyes in death. What was the reason he gave himself so little rest?

It was because he was directed by the Lord to work, and because it was the Lord's work he was doing. Now, you have the same reason for diligence and painstaking in your work that St. Paul had in his. He was told to work by a voice from heaven. "He was not unmindful of the heavenly vision." You too have been told by a voice from heaven—the voice of the Holy Ghost—"Whatsoever ye do, do it from the heart, as to the Lord, and not to men. Knowing that ye shall receive from the Lord the reward of inheritance. Serve ye the Lord Christ" (Col. iii. 24).

This is the thought of all thoughts to be kept ever before the mind; which will give you strength and courage to do all that we should do, and to do it in the very best way.

Take, for example, a girl who has work to do from morning till night. Early in the morning of a washing-day she wakes up. There is a heap of clothes to wash; there is breakfast to get, and, it may be, the chief part of the work of a family to do. It will require all her time and strength to do it. When she wakes up it seems a dismal prospect to her. "Oh, dear! how I shall have to slave it to-day!"

But now the thought comes, "For Jesus Christ, oh! do it cheerfully for His sake." In an instant she is out of bed. "Oh, yes!" she says, "I could not be better employed." She draws water, makes the fire, fills her kettles; there is not a bit of sulkiness or grumbling about it. One thing goes off after another. It is astonishing how this thought makes her do everything so easily and so well. Her appetite is good; and at night she goes to bed full of good health, and with the best conscience in the world. Ah! this is the girl who has got the grand secret.

Yes, my dear girls, if you want to be good and happy, be diligent. Make it a point of conscience not to neglect your work, nor to do it in a lazy or careless way. It is a matter of conscience, for when you receive wages you are bound to give your labor in return. Look into a factory where hundreds of people are as busy as bees, and even there you will find many idlers. They say to themselves, "I don't mean to kill myself working; I shall only get a day's wages any how"; so they dawdle over their work as much as they dare. Others, who are paid by the actual work they do, slight it all they can, so as to get along faster and make a little more money at the end of the week. This is not true diligence, but dishonest haste. You are bound to discharge the duty or office you take upon yourself in a perfect manner, or as it is expected that it should be done.

And as the Lord will reward you for a faithful and diligent performance of it, so He will call you to account and judge you if you neglect it. This is why the Scripture says we must not be "eye-servants."

What is an eye-servant? It is one, if I understand it, who does her duty when the employer's eye is upon her, but who neglects it when her back is turned. One who is very plausible to one's face; who says, "Oh, yes!" but who cannot be depended upon. Such girls do not care; they love their own ease and comfort more than they love their plain duty, more than they love to please God.

Go into the kitchen where such a girl works. What do you see? Well, you may seldom see it in order. The floor is dirty; unwashed dishes and dirty clothes are lying around, when everything ought to be put away. Breakfast, dinner, and supper are always behind-time.

Then, you find the potatoes half boiled, or the meat burnt so that you cannot eat it. The table is half set. The work is always done in a most slovenly manner, or not done at all.

Such a girl is the occasion of a great deal of sin. She provokes ill-temper and defrauds her employers of what they had a right to expect from her.

The Scripture describes it well: " As vinegar to the teeth and smoke to the eyes, so is the sluggard to him that sent him " (Prov. x. 25).

The mistress goes down into the kitchen; there are her girls sitting down with their hands in their laps, talking with one another, or with an acquaintance that has come in. There they have been a full half-hour, and everything behind-hand. It is enough to ruffle the temper of a saint.

Another girl is always running out to see the girl in the next house, leaving the dinner to take care of itself. Another has chamber-work to do: it is the same; until late in the morning all is in confusion. If the children are to be cared for, the poor little things are not half dressed, they get bruised and thumped because they are not watched and attended to as they ought to be.

If several girls are living together, there is an everlasting strife as to whose business it is to do this or to do that, and half the work is not done, and every now and then the only thing to do is to clear out the whole set and get another. Perhaps some poor innocent girl then has to suffer from the negligence of her companions.

CHAPTER LI.

ADVANTAGES OF DILIGENCE.

DON'T be afraid of labor or trouble. The industrious girl will not have near as much work to do as the lazy and shiftless one. Why? Because she manages so that her work is done with much less trouble. She goes right at it without allowing it ever to get the upper hand of her.

If a good deal is to be done in the morning, she gets things ready over-night. A great many things can be done better then than in the morning. One girl will get up in the morning : there is the fire all out ; no kindling-wood ready; the sticks all wet ; the kettle to be filled with water; the coffee to be ground ; the meat to be chopped; everything to be done. She says, "Dear me! there is no living in such a place as this. I don't know where my head is, I've so much to do."

Another girl, of more orderly habits, has had plenty of time over-night to make all these preparations. She has only to light a match, and in a minute has a good blazing fire ; her breakfast is all ready to put on to cook ; and without a bit of fuss or disturbance of mind it is ready

at the moment.   So, from one year's end to
another, where such a girl is, there is peace
and satisfaction all around, while with the
other there is nothing but trouble and sorrow.

This girl has never too much to do, and does
all well.   The other is half the time overloaded
with work, and does it half, while the rest of her
time she is lazy and idle, and committing sin
right and left; for the old saying is true : "The
devil finds work enough for idle hands to do."
A person who performs her task, whatever it
may be, with diligence and intelligence grows
more and more perfect in it all the time.   Look
into the stores and factories and dress-making
establishments, and these are the girls who are
promoted in time to be the heads of departments,
with others under their charge.   Who ever heard
of an idler gaining promotion in the honest
ranks of labor ?

Where is your true perfection and goodness ?
It is in your work.   You may think it is in your
prayers, or in your hearing Mass, or in Confession, or in Communion.   All these things are
good, all these things are necessary, but your
perfection is in your work.

Do your work well, and do it with the right
intention, because it is your duty, and because it
is God's will you should do it, and you will be
on the shortest road to perfection.   All your

prayers, all your confessions, all your communions, will avail little, if your conscience is not in your work.

In a nice little story I have read lately there is a character called Fanny. Now, Fanny was very pious, a monthly communicant. She said her Rosary every day, and must always be at church, particularly when anything extraordinary was going on. One evening a celebrated man was to preach, and Fanny had set her heart on going. But, as it happened, at that very time company came in, and Fanny's services were necessary; she could not go. Now there was a time of it. All her mildness, all her piety was gone. "She wouldn't stand it, it was too bad!" and so on.

The fact is, Fanny's piety was not very deep. She was, after all, more bent on pleasing herself than on pleasing God. She had an oppor· tunity, by putting up with her disappointment and doing her work cheerfully, to gain more than by hearing a dozen sermons.

St. Zita, in her old age, used frequently to say that "no servant is truly devout who is not laborious; and that a lazy piety, in persons of their condition, is a false piety." She practised it herself up to the letter. Not a single moment of her time was unoccupied. She was always ready, when her own work was done, to help others; and as long as she saw anything left undone about the house, she never considered her task over.

That was the way. Every bit of her work was a prayer to God. It gave her no uneasiness that she could not retire to pray on her knees, or in the church, as long as work was to be done; her readiness, her cheerfulness, her fidelity in work, were all so many sacrifices of sweet odor to God, so many prayers proceeding from such an humble, child-like faith. It was in this way that she brought down on herself those streams of grace that made her finally a saint, to be held in love and veneration throughout the church for all ages.

EXAMPLE.

We have another beautiful example of dili- gence and attention in service in the life of a noble lady, Anne of Montmorency, written by Lady Georgiana Fullerton. The family of this lady were making preparations for her marriage, but she felt called by God to a different state of life—a state in which she could imitate the ex- ample of the Lord Jesus Christ more perfectly.

When she found all her entreaties of no avail, she left her father's house at the tender age of fifteen. No one knew what had become of her. She took the name of Jane Margaret, and hired herself out to a lady in a country village.

The lady was so difficult in her temper that

no other girl could remain with her. All the work fell on Anne to do ; she was chambermaid, cook, and portress at the same time.

Just think of that. A delicate young lady, always waited upon, never obliged to do anything in the way of hard work, of a high education and immense wealth, doing all this work !

And she did it well, too. For ten years she served in the utmost patience and fidelity. She overcame evil with good, so that when her mistress was dying, she called her to her bedside and begged her pardon for all she had made her suffer, and insisted on leaving her the sum of four thousand francs, in addition to her wages. Anne accepted it after some hesitation, and gave it all to the poor.

Think over this example, and get from it all the good it teaches so eloquently. If you, born of poor parents and used to hard work, complain and neglect your duties, and pass your time in idleness, let the thought of this delicate and refined lady, working so patiently in the kitchen so many years, shame you into better sentiments. Let it encourage you to overcome your natural weakness and the snares of the devil, until you acquire habits of industry and of faithful attention to your duties. Make this attempt in order to please God, and ask His help. He will not fail to give you abundant grace to accomplish it.

CHAPTER LII.

ON HONESTY.

THERE is one golden sentence of Holy Scripture which ought to be deeply impressed on the heart of every girl who aims at making progress in the love of God. It is this: "But having food and raiment, let us be therewith content" (1 Tim. vi. 8). I call it a golden sentence because it expresses so well the limits a good Christian should put to his desires if he would enjoy true contentment of mind.

Would that we could all of us be satisfied, when God supplies the reasonable wants of the body without craving and worrying for those things which are not required, and which we are, for the most part, much better without.

If we have enough food to keep us in good health and strength, and clothes to keep us decent and warm, we have all that we can make use of. The rest is superfluous, and when life has gone by, even if it lasts ninety years, we shall come to its end, not a bit better for all of it. As Scripture says: "We brought nothing into this world, and it is certain we can carry nothing out" (1 Tim. vi. 7).

The practical meaning of being content with

food and raiment is, that each one should be satisfied with that portion of this world's goods which God assigns him, without repining and fretting because he has not more, and without taking any unjust means to get more. "For covetousness is the root of all evils, which some desiring have erred from the faith, and entangled themselves in many sorrows" (1 Tim. vi. 10).

We are very apt to regard life and happiness as consisting in the possession of those superfluous goods, called riches. It is not so. Riches are very often but sorrows which entangle us, and snares which entrap us into the captivity of the devil. "How hardly shall they that have riches enter into the kingdom of God" (St. Mark x. 23).

If any have cause to complain of God, it is not the poor, but the rich ; for their chance of salvation is the worst. But no one has any right to complain. God distributes riches just as he pleases, and makes it best for each one to be just as he is : the rich to be rich, and the poor to be poor. The rich can be poor in spirit, and the poor rich in faith ; and that will bring all things right for both rich and poor.

And God, having fixed matters in this way, will not allow the poor to steal away the goods of the rich. "Thou shalt not steal" (Ex. xx. 15) is the commandment which applies to all, and which no one is at liberty to transgress. If you have food and raiment you must be contented with it; and if your neighbor has a thousand times more than this of all kinds of luxuries, and conveniences enough for years on years, you cannot reach out your hand to steal the smallest thing of his. This is the will of God; and His commandment, "Thou shalt not steal," stands like a wall of iron against it.

I wish I could impress on each heart, so that it would never be forgotten, the necessity of perfect honesty in all things, small and great. It is difficult to perceive the evils likely to arise from the least want of principle in this respect. St. Paul expresses it very well when he says, "Covetousness is the root of all evils."

From this root grows loss of character and happiness here, and loss of heaven hereafter. The love of money and possessions is so captivating, that when it has once taken root it is hard to pull it up from the heart. It grows stronger and stronger, until it takes up all the room in the heart, and leaves no place for the love of God.

One would think that it would die away in old age and disappear; it is so foolish to be taken up with perishable and valueless things; but no, it grows stronger and stronger to the very grave. For a handful of yellow dirt the soul is sold to the devil, and that dirt has to be left behind. "We can carry nothing out."

How often it involves loss of happiness and character in this world! A girl has a good character. She is esteemed. She can easily get her living and have all she wants. But she begins to pilfer. It goes on from one thing to another, from small to great, until she is detected and disgraced.

The only way is, to stop at the very beginning; to refrain from taking a pin's worth. Have this principle, and there is no danger.

I dare say you have heard the story of the young man who was condemned to be hanged for robbery, and who called to his old mother, as he stood under the gallows, to come up to him, as he had a word to whisper in her ear. She came up, sobbing and crying, when he, instead of saying anything to her, bit off her ear.

"O my son!" she cried, "what have I done that you should serve me so cruelly?" "It is," he replied, "for your cruelty to me in not correcting me for my first theft. If, instead of rewarding me for it, you had given me a sound whipping, I should have taken warning in time. That first theft has brought me to the gallows."

So, a little tea, or a little coffee or sugar, or an article of clothing of not much value, has brought many a poor girl to the loss of character, and the loss of her soul. Many a weak, foolish girl, who has stood at a counter selling articles of finery, would have been horrified when she took that first bit of ribbon if she could have seen the long line of pilferings that were to follow, until she stood a convicted thief behind prison bars. Give no heed to the devil who tempts; who says, "Oh! it is not much, nobody will miss it; the owner is rich, and has more than he knows what to do with; you are poor, and it will do you good"; but give heed to God, who says, "Thou shalt not steal," and "Neither thieves, nor the covetous, nor the unjust," etc., "shall enter the kingdom of Heaven" (1 Cor. vi. 10).

We have a most fearful warning in the case of the Apostle Judas, who sold our Lord for thirty pieces of silver. How did he get so far as to betray his Lord and Master? It was just in this way: by little and little. He let a covetous spirit have its way, first, in small things.

He carried the bag in which the alms were placed which good people gave for the support of the Saviour and the Apostles. He looked with greedy eyes upon them, and began to pilfer what he thought would not be missed. That cursed, avaricious feeling took root and grew in his heart, until he even bargained to betray the Lord Jesus Christ for thirty poor miserable pieces of silver.

CHAPTER LIII.

CONTINUATION.

IS not the same thing done nowadays? A girl comes to Confession. Everything goes on well enough until it comes out that she has stolen something of considerable though not very great value. She is admonished of the necessity of returning that amount, but absolutely refuses. She says, "I cannot." "Why can you not?" says the confessor. "Because I do not wish to." "But have you not the means of doing it?" "Yes," is the reply, "but I don't want to part with the money." "But you cannot be forgiven unless you do; God's law will not allow it." She rises to go. "Stop," says the confessor, "will you lose your soul for a trifling sum of money?" It seems so, for she persists, and goes away sorrowful. Money is more attractive to her than the grace of God, or the kingdom of heaven; like the young man who, when told by the Saviour to sell his goods and follow Him, would not do it, but went away in sadness.

I wish this were only a description of fancy. Alas! such cases have happened. And when the amount is greater, the difficulty of making good the theft becomes almost too great to be overcome.

How many hundreds and thousands give up the grace of God rather than give up those darling dollars they have unjustly acquired ! It is this obligation to restore or give back what is wrongfully taken which makes the sin of theft so dangerous to our salvation. Other sins are forgiven when we are truly sorry and determined to commit them no more : but this is not enough when something has been stolen. If it be a thing of notable value, it must be given back when one has the ability to do so. Of course, so long as one has not the means it cannot be done, and God does not require an impossibility ; but as soon as one has the means the obligation revives.

In this way a sin of theft may be hanging over one's head the greater part of a life-time, causing immense uneasiness and trouble of conscience. Old men and women are often laden with the dishonesty of their youth. They have not been able to make restitution, or they have neglected to do so when they were, and now they see no prospect of ever doing it. They fear to appear before God while it is undone.

How much better, then, to keep one's conscience entirely clear, that we may say at once : '' As for dishonesty, I am entirely set against it, and would not for the world touch a penny's worth of anything not my own.''

Do you know what comparison has often been in my mind when a girl accuses herself of taking little things? I think of a rotten apple. No matter how small a speck of rottenness there is in an apple, it destroys its value. That speck is sure to spread, soundness no longer belongs to that apple.

So the heart which displeases God by pilfering is specked; it is sound no longer. It is not that true heart it ought to be, and most likely that unsoundness or rottenness will spread until the whole heart becomes corrupt. On the contrary, how beautiful it is to observe justice in one's dealings, to be perfectly reliable at all times and under all circumstances. It makes up for a great many other faults.

CHAPTER LIV.

ADVANTAGES OF HONESTY.

HOW often ladies, in talking about their servants, will go over a list of faults, and wind up by saying : '' But, after all, she is as honest as the day. I have never had reason to suspect anything in the shape of stealing or pilfering.'' And all who listen get a favorable opinion.

This is expressed well in the old familiar

maxim : " Honesty is the best policy." One
may acquire some little gain by cheating or
stealing, for a short while, but in the long run
he will gain a great deal more by strict honesty.
So girls will get better places and better wages
as soon as they have an established character
for being strictly honest.

These, however, are only considerations of
this world ; there are vastly more important
ones ; the approval of God in heaven ; the testi-
mony of a good conscience. What kind of a
conscience can a thief or a pilferer have ? A
very bad one, and a very uneasy one. And
this uneasy conscience destroys peace, and when
peace departs, ill-temper and peevishness set in.
One cannot say his prayers with satisfaction.
It is all down-hill with good resolutions and
piety.

Could we only see how much we stand in
our own light by this vice, I am sure we should
detest it from the bottom of our hearts. And,
after all, what is gained ? A small sum of
money, a trifling article of dress or ornament,
something to eat or drink, which gives no satisfaction when we have it. It is the devil who
cheats and deludes us under false pretences, that
he may hold us in a most miserable and galling
slavery.

On the other hand, what a blessed satisfaction the just man, the man who respects his

neighbor's goods out of love to God, enjoys! The Scripture describes it: "Lord, who shall dwell in Thy tabernacle, and rest in Thy holy mountain? He that walketh without blemish and worketh justice" (Ps. xiv. 1). Again, it is said in another psalm: "Who shall ascend into the mountain of the Lord? or who shall stand in His holy place?" The answer is: "The innocent in hands and clean of heart" (Ps. xxiii. 4). Yes, those whose hearts are set to do right, and whose hands are innocent of all picking and stealing.

If we desire an example from Holy Scripture to show how dear to God the man is who is set against all dishonesty, we have the instance of Zaccheus the Publican. When he fell at the Saviour's feet and exclaimed: "Lord, if I have done any man wrong I return him fourfold," the Saviour immediately replied: "This day is salvation come to this house" (St. Luke xix. 8, 9).

What speech more consoling and delightful than this could mortal man desire to hear from the lips of the Lord of eternal glory! Set not, then, your hearts on riches at all. Be content with your living, and God, who clothes the lilies of the field, will see that you have food and clothing. You can earn your honest wages, and be satisfied with them. They will and must suffice for all your desires. In short, be poor in spirit, that is, according to the explanation in the Bible, humble, and not set upon riches, but upon pleasing God, and yours will be the kingdom of heaven.

Why, the very first words of our Saviour in His Sermon on the Mount are these: ''And opening His mouth, He taught them, saying: 'Blessed are the poor in spirit, for theirs is the kingdom of heaven'" (St. Matt. v. iii). Remember these words as long as you live, and carry them out in your life.

CHAPTER LV.

DIFFERENT KINDS OF DISHONESTY.—WASTEFULNESS.

ONE sort of dishonesty is wastefulness, which consists in a want of consideration for the property committed to one's charge. Such waste may amount in value to very large sums of money in the long run. Many a family has been brought to ruin through a wasteful kitchen.

Suppose you know the place where small change, sixpences and five-cent pieces, are kept, and every little while you go there and take a handful to toss among the dirt; you can easily imagine what a havoc you would make with the income of the family.

Well, what is the difference, when you frequently destroy a shilling's worth of butter, or five cents' worth of tea or sugar; when you spoil a batch of bread by your negligence, allow milk and meat to spoil, or throw away victuals which can readily be put to a good use? Is not this scattering money right and left?

You have no right to do so. You are bound to take as much care of the things entrusted to you as if they were your own, and even more. If they were your own, you might have more liberty to dispose of them; but as it is, you are bound by justice towards those whom you have engaged to serve, and who recompense you for taking that care.

And whether they be rich or whether they be poor, does not alter the obligation. If it be a company, a corporation, or the government whom you serve, its property must be none the less sacred in your hands. It is the devil who puts it into your mind that it is of no consequence in such cases. He says: "Oh! never mind; you need not be so particular, they are rich; a little more or a little less is nothing to them." The Blessed Saviour never thought of making any such exception. He expects faithfulness from you in all cases. You are His stewards; all that is entrusted to your care He regards as His own, no matter who the owner may be. And if He sees that you look at it in that light you will be very dear to Him.

Of St. Zita it is said, that although she was so engrossed with prayer, and thinking of God and heavenly things, she never neglected a duty, never suffered anything to go to waste by her negligence.

You remember that beautiful parable of the Lord's, about the servants coming to give account of what they had done with their lord's talents entrusted to them. One, with ten talents, had gained ten others. One, with five, had gained five others. They were rewarded abundantly. Then came the one who had hid his lord's talent in the ground, and he was punished. So it is with servants. Some make good use of all that comes in their hands. They shall be rewarded. Others are wasteful, extravagant, destructive. They shall be punished by the Lord. For we are to do service as to the Lord, and not as man-pleasers.

Be not, then, eye-servants, doing your duty when your employer's eye is upon you ; but remember that the Lord's eye sees you. Take care, take pains, use all the discretion and judgment God has given you ; for it is not merely the·hands, but the head also, which you must use in your daily tasks. Be in all respects like a prudent and careful owner in regard to his own property, and look to the Lord for your recompense. In this way you shall not fail in the great day to reap an abundant recompense, according to the Lord's promise : '' Inasmuch as ye have done it unto the least of these, ye have done it unto me '' (St. Matt. xxv. 40).

CHAPTER LVI.

DISHONESTY ON THE PRETEXT OF CHARITY.

THERE are various ways of taking another's property to one's own use, that have a kind of blind or cover over them which tends to conceal their real guilt. The devil is always ready to bring these excuses to mind.

One is : ''Oh ! I have only given away to poor people something that wouldn't amount to much : a few grains of sugar, or a little tea ; a lump of butter, or some victuals that wouldn't be missed ; a few old clothes, a worn-out table-cloth, or some half-worn towels, and so on.''

This covers a good deal. I dare say you have heard of smuggling—that is, secretly getting goods from other countries without paying the duties, and so selling them cheap. Large fortunes are sometimes made in this way. The practice of smuggling away goods out of the house you live in, perhaps to a mother, a sister, or a neighbor, covers often a brisk trade, which if it were all summed up would make a large amount.

It goes on quietly but continually. It is like the circle made by a stone thrown in the water, that enlarges all the while. It is petty thieving, and deserves no better name. It may wear the cloak of charity, but it is not the less stealing. If one makes himself master of another's goods without his consent, he steals; it makes no difference whether he keeps them for his own use or gives them away.

Objects of real charity may present themselves; they may beg you to help them; they may ask for this or that which they see you have in charge; but you should never let them have anything unless you first go and get the authority of the owner. It is a temptation, I know, for a poor girl who has a widowed mother or sister to help, when she sees plenty around her that will be so acceptable to them, and will not be missed; but it is a temptation of the enemy of souls, a very great snare for her ruin. Turn a deaf ear to all such temptations.

Turn a deaf ear to every so-called friend who tries to coax or flatter you, or to work on your kind feelings, to make you fall into this snare. Say: "Not a penny's worth will I give away."

Do as St. Zita did. A more benevolent,

kind-hearted creature than she was could not be; she never refused any poor person, but mind you, it was not at her master's expense. She saved her own wages. She denied herself many a thing to eat, many a thing to wear, and gave that to the poor.

Oh, how pleasing such charity is to God! It observes the everlasting precepts of justice out of regard and respect to Him, and relieves the poor of Christ at the same time.

But the other kind of charity is no charity at all. It is robbing your own souls to give to others' bodies. It is outraging and offending God on the pretence of doing Him service.

Make it then your rule, and keep to it, to give away nothing that you do not own yourself, or which you are not clearly authorized to give away. So will you avoid a world of trouble and a disturbed and doubtful conscience.

CHAPTER LVII.

DISHONESTY ARISING FROM GLUTTONY.

SOMETIMES a sort of dishonesty arises from gluttony, from too great desire to enjoy expensive and delicate food. One is not satisfied with ordinary fare, but is all the time looking out for this or that which they fancy will gratify their palate. This leads them to take those things they have no sort of right to, such as cakes, sweetmeats, wines, or liquors.

Many families, who have such things, cannot afford to make them common. They keep them in places under their own control, and for extraordinary occasions. Even the children of the house have no use of them, except by permission. Now, it is, of course, entirely wrong secretly to get hold of and consume such things.

The fact that they are not taken out of the house or given away, but eaten or drunk at home, does not make it less a robbery; for it is well understood that they are entirely removed from your control.

You might as well take money or other things as to take these. And if it be in the houses of the wealthy that these delicacies or expensive things are reserved, it makes no difference ; they are as much out of your reach as if in another's house.

You are entitled to good, wholesome food, and in sufficient quantity to keep up full health and strength. When you have this, you ought to be contented.

I believe domestics in this country have in general very little to complain of in this respect. They share in pretty much all that is in use in the family, and have a diet good enough for any one. If here and there an exception is made and something is kept back, it is only reasonable it should be so.

But it is really too bad when a girl is always complaining of her food, wanting to cook something for herself different from that which is in use in the family, and so making a deal of trouble and vexation.

On Fridays, in Protestant families, there may be room for exception where nothing but meat is provided ; but even here it is more edifying and more Catholic, if we cannot readily provide something special or one is refused permission to do so, to get along with bread and butter, or vegetables, or some such substantial food, than to make a great matter of it.

I like very much the remark of an author, who says that domestics should accustom themselves to a very plain and simple diet, and that even if they live in places where the food is delicate and rich, they should avoid allowing themselves to set much store by it. It may very well happen that after living on rich food for some time they may be disgusted at having to take up with what is plainer and more suitable.

Plain diet is best for every one. It is hurtful for kings, queens, rich and noble, to gratify the palate. It ruins health and it ruins peace of mind. We cannot be servants of Jesus Christ and of the belly at the same time.

Nothing destroys the delight of the soul in heavenly things more quickly than this love of eating and drinking. So the Saviour says: "Take heed to ourselves lest perhaps your hearts be overcharged with surfeiting (*i.e.*, over-eating) and drunkenness, and the cares of this life and that day come upon you suddenly" (St. Luke xxi. 34).

You remember, I dare say, the parable of the rich man and the poor beggar who sat at his gate. Now, all that is said of the rich man is that his thoughts and time were taken up in feasting and living sumptuously. It is not said that he committed other crimes, yet when he died his soul went into hell. No doubt he was guilty of deadly sins, but they are not mentioned, because they grew out of his love of pleasure, which was the root of them and caused his damnation.

Oh, then, avoid this sin! According to the Gospel rule, having food and raiment, having sufficient for your health and strength, be contented with it; desire nothing more, and be careful not to set your heart on more, if it come in your way.

Imitate the example of so many of the holy men and women whom the Church has canonized. Of Blessed Sebastian of Apparizio it is related, that when the daughter of his employer used to make cake and pies to present to him, he would never eat them. He said such kind of food was not suitable for a farm-servant, but not knowing how to refuse without giving offence, and at a loss what to do with them, he gave them to the cows and horses. Many of the saints would rather do this than pamper their own appetites with delicate food.

How poor and plain has been the diet of many a high-born lady, whose heart has been pierced with the desire to live for God and His love alone! Of St. Frances of Rome, we read that from a very early age she practised very great abstinence in regard to food. Nothing but water was ever drank by her. She ate no meat, eggs, or any sweet things, but simply boiled vegetables and bread. After her marriage to one of the richest and noblest men of Rome, when she had to sit at the head of a splendid table with every luxury upon it, she carried out the same mode of life; but so quietly and modestly that very few noticed her, or, if they did, thought it owing to her peculiar state of health.

Of another holy woman, Anne of Montmorency, of one of the best families of France, we know that for a long time she lived on what she could beg at the church-door from day to day; then on a little bread and water which she got twice a week by begging; and at last on the wild fruits and vegetables she collected in the woods. How such examples ought to shame us, who think so much on our stomachs and so little on the good of our souls!

To sum up, then: be perfectly satisfied with a good and sufficient diet, no matter how plain it may be; and for the love of God not lay dishonest hands on anything eatable or drinkable out of a spirit of gluttony.

CHAPTER LVIII.

DISHONESTY ON THE PRETEXT OF INSUFFICIENT WAGES.

DO not let the devil delude you with another false pretence. He may say to you that you do not get enough wages; that other girls are getting more, who do not work more than you do, and that you are justified in helping yourself, if you can, to what will make up the difference.

Or, he may whisper in your ear that your work is harder than usual, or that you work a longer time than other girls, and that you should have something for it; and that you might as well take something when you see your chance.

Now, all these are truly devilish suggestions. Take the wages you have agreed to serve for and be satisfied. It may be a little more or a little less, but it is what you agreed for.

A bargain is a bargain. When you make a bargain and benefit by it, you are glad enough to get that benefit; and others think as you do when they make a close bargain. You have no right to make a bargain unless you intend to hold to it. If you have not been aware of all the facts of the case, try to make a better bargain; and if you do not succeed, then you are at liberty, after due notice, to go somewhere else.

It is a wide door of sin to undertake to recompense yourself on any plea of low wages or extra work. If such excuses were once allowed there would be no such thing as putting confidence in any agreement.

The merchant would cheat, delivering not what he agreed to, but what he pleases. The tailor would cheat in his clothing, putting in worse material and work than he agreed upon, and pocketing the difference. He would say: "Oh! I give them pretty nigh the worth of their money, and that is all that can be expected of me." The carpenter and the mason would do just as they pleased. "Oh! the material I put in is not what I agreed to, but it is good enough; I don't make any more than I ought to." The milliner and the dressmaker would cheat. The world would be filled with deceit and fraud of the basest and meanest kind. The dishonest thief would carry on his thieving operations under the cloak of a saint: "Oh! I do no wrong; I am entitled in justice to all I have taken."

God in Heaven cannot abide such practices. Listen to what St. John the Baptist has preached on the subject: "He said therefore to the multitudes that came to be baptized by him: Ye offspring of vipers, who has showed you to flee from the wrath to come? Bring forth, then, fruit worthy of penance." And the people asked him, What shall we do? He replied and told them what to do. Then the publicans asked him the same question. He told them also. But when the soldiers asked, What shall we do? He replied: "Do violence to no man, neither calumniate any man"; and remark well what else: "Be content with your pay" (St. Luke iii. 14); that is, do not plunder and steal on the plea of having too little pay. The soldiers are here threatened with the wrath of God if they should undertake to increase their gains beyond the wages they had agreed upon.

In the same way the wrath of God will fall on the person in these days who increases his pay by secret means. Such suggestions are like false teachers, "wolves in sheeps' clothing." They are ravening wolves, never satisfied, but attacking one thing after another, until they have devoured every bit of goodness and virtue in you. Wherever you may be employed or whatever your work may be resist, then, with fortitude every such temptation.

If money passes through your hands in buying or selling, use no fraud or deceit about the price, but give back every cent of change. Sell nothing out of the house, nothing whatever, no matter what others may do or say. Accept no presents or bribes from storekeepers, or any one else, to cover up any dishonest transaction. Come down, completely and simply, to your pay, and be content therewith, that you may flee from the wrath to come, and commend yourselves as truly honest servants in whom there is no guile.

CHAPTER LIX.

CO-OPERATION IN DISHONESTY.

THERE is another snare to be avoided which is sometimes very dangerous. It arises from the sins of others. You have associates who are dishonest, and who want to make use of you to carry on their designs. If they do not want this, they at least want to get you mixed up in the same kind of business so that they may not be told of, or because an unquiet conscience gets some consolation in the thought that others are as bad as themselves.

No matter what the motive may be that leads them to drag you into their dishonesty, have nothing whatever to do with it.

But suppose it is a person who has the confidence of the head of the establishment, who carries things as he pleases, and he or she threatens to get you turned out if you do not do as they wish you. Never mind ; suffer yourselves to be turned out of the place, but do not steal.

Even if it be a child in the family, a brother or a sister of your employer, or a fellow-clerk, have nothing to do with their wickedness. If it be a partner in any business in which you are employed who is stealing from his partner, and who threatens or coaxes you, give no heed to him.

Even if you are threatened with being accused of stealing yourself, or with having slanderous stories set afloat about you by wicked persons, out of spite and malice, do not be moved an inch from the right course. Have nothing to do with their wickedness.

God will reward you for all you have to suffer. He will make the right appear in good time, and all your sufferings will be rich crowns of merit for you. " Blessed are you when men revile you and persecute you falsely for My sake, and for justice' sake. Rejoice and be exceeding glad, for great shall be your reward in heaven " (St. Matt. v. 11).

The question may be asked : " If I know of another's stealing and I have nothing to do with it myself, am I obliged to make it known ? It is a thing I should not like to do, for nothing seems meaner than to be telling of others."

We cannot always do just what we like ; we

must do what the law of God requires.   As St.
Paul says: " But as for me it is a thing of the
least account to be judged by you or by human
judgment,   .   .   .   but He that judgeth me is
the Lord " (1 Cor. iv. 3).

In truth, there is nothing mean, nothing dishonorable in informing when wickedness is going on, and your information will stop it.   It
requires courage, it is true, but that makes it
the more noble and more full of merit.

In most cases you are bound, through many
motives, to give information.

It is your duty to your employers, a duty of
charity and often of justice.   If you are in
charge of certain things and responsible for
their safe-keeping, and allow them to be taken,
you would be bound in justice to take means to
prevent their being stolen ; and if you did not,
you would be under obligation to make good
the loss.

If you are not in such a position, it is a duty
of charity, at least, to inform and prevent the
evil from going on.   You are, for the time being, a member of the family ; and can you believe that you can fold your arms and let robbery go on without trying to prevent it ?   The
very idea is monstrous ; it is contrary to the
first principles of conscience.

Then it is a duty you owe yourself.   If you
do not inform, you run a great risk of losing

your own character. When it is discovered, as it will very likely be, and it is known that you were aware of it and did not tell, you will be almost sure to be considered as an accomplice in the crime. Your character is valuable to you, and it is your duty to preserve it, and you have no right to expose it to so great a risk of being lost.

Charity to innocent persons who may be unjustly suspected or accused requires that the real offender be known.

And finally, it is a charity to the dishonest persons. It is far better for them to be found out and punished than to be allowed to go on hardening themselves and increasing in guilt all the while. The rule is, then, in spite of all your dislike, to do your duty and reveal their sin.

Are there no exceptions to this rule? Undoubtedly there are. Let us see what they are.

If they should be violent persons, of a slanderous tongue and willing to do you mischief in revenge for telling of them, would that excuse you? I think not. As I said before, your reputation is in the hands of God, who will see to it that all turns out well for you. They will not hurt you. You will come out of such trials like gold purified in the fire, very lovely in the eyes of men for your solid virtue, and in God's all-seeing eye for your faithfulness to Him, though at the cost of some suffering. But suppose your information will do no good, but only get yourself into trouble? In that case you are not under any obligation to reveal.

The guilty persons may be so much in the confidence of the employer as to be able to throw suspicion off themselves on you and injure you seriously. No obligation of charity to others can outweigh that of justice to yourself and your own reputation. It is well in such case to get prudent advice and act upon it.

CHAPTER LX.

PRACTICAL DIRECTIONS IN THIS MATTER.

NOW, how ought you to proceed in case you have to inform your employers of the thefts of others? That depends a good deal on their characters and dispositions. If they be prudent persons, whom you could rely on to treat the guilty parties with mercy and justice, to keep the information secret, and screen you from being known to have exposed the matter, tell them at once and let them take their measures. But a great many employers are not of this character. They are hasty and violent and inconsiderate of others. In that case you must use precautions.

1st. Confine yourself at first to making known the bare fact of the theft. Say that such or such a thing has disappeared, that you have remarked that things have disappeared from time to time, or that at least they were there at such a time and you have missed them since; that you had thought it your duty to warn them in order that they might take means accordingly.

2d. If your employers ask you the proofs of what you say, give them, but keep back, if you can, the name of the guilty party. If that is impossible, give the name, but with pity and compassion for her or them, and begging that they may be treated with indulgence.

3d. Ask that they will find out for themselves and not take things on your word. Say you are willing to be watched as well as the rest; that you only wished to put them on their guard and leave the rest to them.

4th. If they desire to put you in the position of spying out and collecting evidence against the suspected person, refuse any such office; at least, unless the nature of your service obliges you to it. This is the only case in which it is your duty to act as a spy on others, and it is only *duty* that should be powerful enough to make you do any such thing. In your position, too, you can hardly keep yourself disinterested and peaceable and calm enough to undertake such a thing ; and your employers will, if they are reasonable, not insist upon it, but rather admire your conduct in declining it. Ask that what you have told may be kept secret, for you do not wish to be exposed to the enmity and persecution that would fall upon you if it were known that you had given information about the matter.

Good sense and prudence point out some such rules, in case you are bound in conscience to give information ; and good sense and prudence will teach even the most ignorant how to proceed.

A poor old negro man came to a priest not long ago. "Father," says he, "I want you to advise me. You told me when I saw anything going to loss to tell massa. Now, the other day I saw something going to loss. I didn't want to tell of anybody ; but my conscience told me I ought to tell massa something was going to loss. So, says I, Massa, when you go around the farm and come to such a place, you just keep your eye skinned, and see if you don't see something going to loss. So massa, he look out bright, and see what was going on, and he hauled 'em up for it.

"Then they comes to me and 'cuses me of telling of 'em. And I says, I didn't tell of anything. Now, did I do right?"

What a wonderful prudence and charity this

simple old man showed! Try and follow his example.

Do not run, neither, to inform in an excess of zeal, when the matter is very trifling and when also you have a mere suspicion without positive proof. You have charity to your fellow-servants to exercise as well as charity to your employers. Guard against all malice and spite, and purify your motives so that it may be a pure conscience that actuates you, and that all may be done for God and for God alone.

CHAPTER LXI.

ON SPYING AND LISTENING.

IT is not merely a thing of the utmost importance to be faithful in respect to the property of your employers, but also in regard to their character and reputation. In order to do this, in the first place, you must be on your guard against idle curiosity and keep your mind from desiring to know their secret affairs, as well as your eyes and ears from spying them out or listening to them.

It is not merely improper and unbecoming to do so, but it is a sin. Their private and family affairs are their own. They expect no one to meddle with them. It is the same thing with regard to conversation with their friends and acquaintances, the letters they write, and so on. They would feel offended if they knew that you were curious enough even to pay attention to such things ; and much more, if they knew you had taken any means to spy them out. It stands to reason, then, that it is wrong to do so; and I know it is against the voice of your conscience, which warns you that you have no business with such things.

Scripture tells us the same thing in the strongest language. St. Paul says : '' For we have heard that there are some among you who walk disorderly, working not at all, but curiously meddling. Now we charge them that are such, and beseech them by the Lord Jesus Christ, that working with silence they would eat their own bread '' (2 Thess. iii. 11, 12).

It is no wonder the holy Apostle begs and entreats, for where there is this vain itching spirit of prying into other people's business there can be little piety. When one is taken up with affairs of this world which are none of his business, what time or heart can he have for the great affair of his salvation? When his head is full of the most useless and hurtful trash of other people's, what room is there for the quiet and peaceable spirit of God? The ''eyes of a fool are in the ends of the earth,'' says the Holy Scripture (Prov. xvii. 24).

This vain, idle spirit of curiosity leads to numerous sins. It leads to idle gossip; it leads to detraction; it leads to quarrels and dissension; it leads straight to the ruin of the soul, as it led our first mother, Eve, as we all know, to eat the forbidden fruit. Do not follow, then, your first mother Eve's example, but put away all this itching curiosity.

When you go upstairs to sweep lay no curious eyes on anything which seems to contain a secret. Pry into no drawers or closets that are kept closed. Take no inventories of articles which you have no concern with. When letters are lying about do not read them. If they are open before you, rather tear out your eyes than do the mean, low-lived trick of reading them.

Do not creep up, like a guilty thief, to listen behind doors when conversation is going on. And, more than this, if you are where you can overhear anything private, go away or make some noise which will give warning of your presence, so that such conversation may be conducted more privately.

Do as you would do if you were where you were likely to overhear a secret of the sacred tribunal of Confession. Stop your ears to all such things; pay no attention to them when they are overheard. Have no time for such things, as the Apostle admonishes: '' But we entreat you, brethren, that you abound more

and that you use your endeavors to be quiet and
to mind your own business, and work with your
hands as we have commanded you, and that
you want nothing of any man's" (1 Thess. iv.
10, 11).

So will your time and all your mind be clear
and free to abound more and more in the science
and knowledge of Jesus Christ, who is a well of
knowledge and of love and goodness sufficient
to occupy all your thoughts and satisfy all your
desires. Ah! this is the curiosity, this is the
study which has no limit, which has nothing
but what is lovely and pure and good in it.

CHAPTER LXII.

OBLIGATION OF SECRECY.

THIS vain curiosity about the affairs of your
employers leads by a short way to another
very great evil, and that is, to revealing and
making known to people abroad those things
which ought to be kept in the house. A person curious enough to want to find out such
things will prove a leaky vessel. She will not
rest until she has talked it over with her friends
and acquaintances. Everything that goes on in
the house will be made a subject of discussion.
The conduct of the mistress towards her husband, or his towards her; the conversations be-

tween them or other members of the family at
the table ; what persons have visited the house,
and what was overheard of their conversation ;
the money-affairs, courtships, spats and quarrels of the family, will all be retailed, like so
many choice morsels, for the amusement of
one's self and friends.

It may be sins or faults of character will be
spread about, dressed up in such a way that
they have quite a different look from the reality. As Scripture says : " And without being
idle, they learn to go about from house to
house ; not only idle, but tattlers also, and in-
quisitive, speaking things they ought not "
(1 Tim. v. 13).

All this is wrong ; it is a violation of that
agreement which must always exist between
employers and their dependents. When you
entered their house they committed to you, of
course and of necessity, many things relating
to their private lives, and it was understood
that these things were sacred ; not to go out of
the house ; to be buried in silence.

It was something like the agreement between
the priest and his penitent. He says nothing
about keeping what he hears secret, but it is as
well understood as if he swore the most solemn
oath. They said, perhaps, nothing about this
duty not to repeat his advice or admonition, but
it was as well understood as if they had.

It is most necessary that it should be so. What mischiefs, what strifes, heart-burnings, suspicions, and sins are not stirred up by such conduct! Such things spread from mouth to mouth, until a whole town almost is involved in numberless sins of the tongue. Character is sometimes destroyed and life rendered a burden.

As Holy Scripture says: "The words of a tale-bearer are as wounds that penetrate to the inmost parts of the bowels" (Prov. xxvi. 22). Hear what the prophet says, speaking of different kinds of the wicked: "Tale-bearers and slanderers have been among thee to shed blood, and they have committed wickedness in the midst of thee" (Ezech. xxii. 9).

God abhors such conduct: " Six things do I hate, and the seventh my soul abhorreth: Haughty eyes, a lying tongue, hands that shed innocent blood, a heart hatching evil thoughts, feet swift to run into mischief, false witnesses bringing out lies" (Prov. vi. 16). What is the seventh that God abominates? *The one who sows strife among brethren.* Who is that one? The tale-bearer, the revealer of secrets. For, if this were to cease, strife and enmity would cease also. "When there is no tale-bearer strife ceaseth" (Prov. xxvi. 20).

But is it right, in any case, to reveal the sins or faults of those who employ you? In answer to this question, I say that, although as a gene-

ral rule it is not right, there are some exceptions. Your own good or that of another may
justify it sometimes.

For example : If you have to leave certain
employers on account of their misconduct or ill-
usage, and your parents or relations, who have
a right to know, inquire the reason, and you
cannot conceal it without mischief, you could
make known why you had to leave.

Or, suppose another girl gets a position in
a place where you have been working and
which is a dangerous one for her; charity
would require that she should be put upon her
guard, and not allowed to run the risk of serious damage to her soul or her character.

A great deal depends on circumstances.
You should be careful not to reveal more than
is necessary, and to take into account the
character of the parties to whom you reveal it,
whether they be prudent and discreet, or light-
headed and rattle-brained persons.

Necessity is the only plea for speaking at all,
and necessity must put the exact limit to what
you speak; otherwise you will run the risk of
doing great wrong and committing great sin.

It is well to take advice of those competent
to give it. Lay open the circumstances of the
case, and abide by the advice given you. And,
above all, lay the matter before God, and ask
the Holy Ghost to guide you.

Purify your motive, and say over and over again to yourself that you will and intend to follow God's holy will in the matter just as far as God shall enlighten you, and not depart a hair's-breadth from it.

In this way you will be sure not to fail. If you make a mistake, it will be no fault of yours, and you will have before God the same merit and the same reward as if you had made none, for God looks at the intention rather than at the success and result of what you do.

CHAPTER LXIII.

ON HOLY PURITY.

WE now come to a subject of the highest importance as respects the eternal salvation of the soul—that is, modesty, or holy purity. St. Alphonsus remarks that the greater number by far of the souls that are lost are damned in consequence of sins against holy purity ; indeed, he says that all, probably, who come to their ruin do so, in some way, through this vice.

The greatest saints, the most holy men and women, have never felt themselves secure against it while life was in their bodies ; but have trembled with fears lest they should fall at last ; and have watched over themselves with untiring vigilance to guard against any such fall.

We are all of flesh and blood, all subject to temptation in this respect; and, therefore, it is most necessary for us all to be exceedingly watchful and full of prayer to God, lest we also fall.

Even St. Paul, the Apostle, after unheard-of labors, and burning zeal, and wonderful prayer says he had to chastise and mortify his body, lest he should lose the fruit of his labor and become reprobate. O dear, precious souls, who really strive to love God! bear this in mind; be full of lively dread and horror of even the least immodesty. Regard it as a horrible monster, ready to devour you if you expose yourself in the least to its power.

That was the way St. Aloysius considered it. When an immodest word was spoken at his father's table by one of the guests he turned as pale as death and came near fainting. He was right; there was a danger to his immortal soul in that word greater than any other kind of danger. His soul trembled at it, as we would shrink and tremble at the roar of a lion were we alone in a dark forest.

Why must we regard it in this light? I will tell you. We are required by the law of God to be perfectly chaste and pure in thought, word, and deed. If we wilfully and deliberately consent to any impurity in these respects, we commit a grievous sin, and of course lose the grace of God. You see how strict the law of God is on one side.

Now, on the other it is needless to say that we carry about with us an inclination to this vice, and it will be impossible not to yield in the time of temptation, unless we constantly strive against it.

How easy, then, is it to commit such sins! Truly, this vice must be regarded as a monster, with jaws wide open to destroy us. It is the very pit of hell which yawns wide at our feet, ready to swallow up those who do not watch their steps with the utmost precaution.

Besides the danger of eternal ruin that attends this sin, it produces the most horrible destruction of all virtue and goodness in the soul. St. Thomas of Villanova describes this well. He says: "When this fire of lust possesses a man it leaves nothing unconsumed. Although he may in his youth have been adorned with the beauty of every virtue, and, like a paradise of God, shining with fragrant and blooming lilies, if once this fire penetrates within his heart, it burns, it consumes all, it reduces all to ashes, and changes him from an agreeable paradise to a horrid desert—from an angel to a beast."

There are some poisons which creep on, when they have once infected the smallest portion of the body, until they leave not a single part of it untouched; they corrupt and destroy until every limb, every organ becomes a loathsome mass of rottenness, so that one would wish himself dead rather than be in such a state.

This is exactly what this horrid vice does to the soul. All goodness, all virtue, all love of God, all faith, hope, or charity, seem to be destroyed by it. As St. Gregory says: "From luxury are generated blindness of heart, inconsideration, inconstancy, heedlessness, love of one's self, hatred of God, supreme attachment to the present world, horror and desperation of the future."

Besides the loss of virtue there is a most fearful loss of peace and happiness. The peace and joy of the pure mind is beyond all description. It is a fountain of pure, living water, flowing from the heart and making everything around green and beautiful.

Take a pure-minded young person; why, the very sight of the innocent mind shining through that modest countenance fills every one who looks upon it with delight. It is like Heaven beaming forth on this earth. There are many such poor boys and poor girls from Ireland whom you love the moment you speak with them, for their innocence and purity of heart. But how this horrid vice destroys all happiness as soon as it has once got entrance into the heart! Where there was a paradise before, there is a hell now. All that peace of mind is gone, leaving distraction, confusion, and trouble to take its place.

Misfortune, sickness, pain, could not have made any such change, but immodesty can; it can destroy all peace and love of God and joy in the soul, and leave nothing but sin and despair.

It destroys oftentimes, also, one's reputation or character, which is and ought to be dearer to us than any worldly goods. Who can live in this world with any pleasure when the finger of scorn is continually pointed at him? who reflects that his disgrace is just, that by his own misconduct he has lost the right to the respect which virtuous persons possess.

How often it has happened to happy, light-hearted young women, happy in the esteem and love of all around them, by yielding to the vice of impurity to lose all this and become a perfect byword and reproach, wretched and miserable, through the loss of that good name without which life is a burden!

Hold, then, this vice in entire abomination, and avoid it in every shape and every form. If you have unfortunately fallen into its power, rise up immediately from it and put it all away, even to the least remnant. In thought, word, and deed maintain entire purity. Apply every reme-dy to get yourself out of the power of this sin.

CHAPTER LXIV.

ON EVIL THOUGHTS.

IN the first place, take care of evil thoughts or imaginations. Thoughts go before actions. If we did not first conceive evil in the mind, we should never commit it in deed. This is what the Scripture says: "For from within, out of the heart of men, proceed evil thoughts, adulteries, fornications, murders, etc. All these evil things come from within and defile a man" (St. Matt. xv. 19, 20).

We have no more right to indulge an evil imagination or thought than to do an evil deed. As soon as we perceive, then, that our minds are dwelling upon a bad thought, we must promptly and firmly strive to drive it away, either by thinking on something else, or by praying to be delivered from it. For example, we may say: "God help me!" "Far be it from me to think of such a thing"; or, what is very good, we may repeat devoutly the holy names of Jesus and Mary, or make the sign of the cross, that holy sign which recalls our hope of salvation and our dread of all that will hinder it.

Many, very many I fear, have no proper idea of the sinfulness and danger of evil thoughts.

They esteem them small matters. They are not small matters; they are very great and very important. I may say salvation depends upon them.

We cannot be in the grace of God, we cannot have a hope of salvation, we cannot live peaceful or pious lives, unless we are set against all bad thoughts; unless we are prepared to drive them from our minds as soon as we discover them.

We cannot always hinder them from entering our minds, because our imaginations or fancies are not always in our power. They may enter in the twinkling of an eye. We may not even notice for a little while what we are thinking about; when, for example, we are perplexed or fatigued or absent-minded. In that case we do not sin because we do not consent to wrong; but as soon as we do take notice and think, " These are sinful imaginations; I must not indulge or take pleasure in them," then we must do as I have just said, put them out at once. By behaving in this way, such evil thoughts can do us no harm; on the contrary, they become a great occasion of merit.

Many pious persons, who hate and detest every sin of impurity and every bad thought, are distressed and annoyed by such things coming in their minds in spite of themselves, and even imagine they have sinned by them. But as long as they hate and detest them, as long as they strive to put them out, their anxiety is entirely ungrounded. We have an instance of this in the life of St. Catherine of Siena. Her soul was assailed by the most horrible temptations of the devil. They lasted a long time, but she resisted, and after the conflict was over our Saviour appeared to her with a serene countenance. "O my Divine Spouse," she said, "where wast Thou when I was enduring these conflicts?" "In thy soul," He replied. "What! with all these filthy abominations?" "Yes, they were displeasing to thee ; this, therefore, was thy merit, and thy victory was owing to My presence."

Do not endeavor to excuse such thoughts on any pretence whatever. Do not say they are natural ; do not think of such things on the idea that you will marry by and by, but simply put them all out and keep them out. When you have closed the door of your heart the enemy cannot find any entrance for evil.

CHAPTER LXV.

CUSTODY OF THE EYES.

IF you will really guard your heart or your thoughts from evil, you must guard your eyes and your ears from seeing or hearing what is evil. The eyes are justly called the windows of the soul. Now, you know, if you stand gazing out of the windows you cannot help thinking of what you see; your mind will become filled with images and pictures of what your eyes behold. So, if you look on any impure sight to notice it, it will be sure to create evil thoughts in your mind.

Perhaps if you had the best will in the world you could not entirely avoid every evil sight, because such things present themselves sometimes suddenly to view; but in that case turn your eyes away immediately with horror, and no impression will be made on your mind. On the other hand, you can readily perceive that to dwell on any evil sight, even for a short time, would produce a considerable impression and be a very evil thing.

For this reason Job, that saint of God, says he made a covenant with his eyes not so much as to look upon a woman. Oh! what a virtue here is, to be so bent on pleasing our Maker as to turn away instantly, not only from every evil sight, but from every dangerous object that may meet our eyes! Such faithfulness renders us very dear to God.

But in order to acquire this modesty of the eyes, it is necessary to restrain them from look- ing at everything that presents itself; to have it habitually at heart to keep down an idle curi- osity to see everything. Downcast eyes accom- pany the chaste spirit, and indicate an inward purity.

Women of true modesty do not gaze here and there fixedly as they walk the streets, but look around, if at all, with a great deal of reserve.

It is, indeed, a hateful and repulsive sight to see the airs of a vain or bold woman. Her whole soul shows itself in her dress, and walk, and eyes, as she goes along, sweeping the streets with her train, with a toss of her head and an affected walk, and her eyes gazing boldly about. Who feels anything but sorrow at the sight? sorrow that an immortal soul should be so per- verted from the intention God had in creating it; sorrow at the spiritual ruin betokened; sor- row that a human being can become so debased. Could such persons see the hearts of those who look at them and read each secret thought re- garding them, they would soon learn to despise themselves and to change their demeanor.

What looks well in a turkey or a peacock, an irrational dumb beast, looks very ugly and unbecoming in a woman with an immortal soul. Be careful, then, of your eyes, how you allow them to gaze about.

St. Francis of Assisi once said to a brother: "Come, brother, let us go out into the city and preach the Gospel." So they went out and walked about a good while, and at last came back to the house without either of them speaking a word. On entering the house again the brother said: "Father Francis, I thought you said we were going out to preach, but here we are again without having opened our mouths." "Brother," says he, "we have preached a most eloquent sermon to all who observed us, by the modest and recollected way in which we have walked the streets of the town."

By the habit of modestly avoiding curious and fixed gazing in the streets, or out of windows in public places, you will avoid a thousand sights which would be dangerous to your souls, although you had no bad intention whatever in such gazing.

CHAPTER LXVI.

OF EVIL CONVERSATIONS.

ALL that has been said in regard to watching carefully the eyes applies as well to the ears and the tongue. There is a vast amount of talk, which we may flatter ourselves is innocent, but which is extremely hurtful to the soul. To speak sometimes of beaux and getting married is, I suppose, unavoidable, and need not have any harm in it ; but it would seem that girls can hardly get together without their conversation being entirely taken up with these things. If they are ever so long with one another, or ever so often, it would seem that this one subject never grows wearisome or gets worn out.

" Well, what harm is there in that ? " A great deal. If nothing worse, it fills the mind with matters too engrossing and enticing to leave us free for the service of God. It is like setting up an idol in our hearts and falling down to worship it, instead of the living and true God. If God condemns the love of riches as idolatry because it distracts and turns us aside from better things, much more must He condemn us for allowing earthly love to occupy and take up our

minds, since this is a passion still more dangerous and powerful to steal our hearts away from
Him.

Such conversations are likely to be hurtful
and evil, even if they do not touch upon anything positively sinful, but how difficult it is to
restrain them within bounds !

"The poison of asps," says St. James, "is
under their lips." The asp was a most deadly
serpent, but very small, and his bite not painful,
so that the person bitten was taken off almost
before he was aware of his wound.

It is this conversation about marriage, this
joking and merriment about beaux, which in-
flicts deadly wounds on the innocent soul so
silently and quietly that it is destroyed almost
before it is aware of its danger.

Keep your tongue from joining in such conversations, and turn away your ears that they
listen not, if you want to escape the infection and
contagion which is all about. Imitate the conduct of physicians who have to attend the sick
in hospitals. They carry with them smelling-
bottles, and the instant they perceive the evil
odor of contagion they strive to counteract it by
breathing the perfume. Turn the conversation
to something else as cunningly as you can; if
you cannot do that, take no part in it and do
not listen to it, but lift up your souls in some
short prayer to God to preserve you. Go away

as soon as you can, so as to be removed from all danger.

The Holy Scripture says that for every "idle word" we shall be called to judgment. Now, by "idle words" is meant, not innocent merriment and cheerful conversation which simply passes away time—for this has a good end, which is to unbend the mind, and prevent melancholy and sadness, and to promote good-feeling and kindness—but just this kind of talk, which seems not so very bad at first sight, but which has the sting and poison of hell in it.

And how is this talk often described? By such expressions as these : "Oh, I have spoken a few pleasant words"; or, "some funny words"; or, "a little joking"; or, "a few double-meaning words." What a fearful stupor of soul and deadness of conscience here is!

"A few double-meaning words!" These double-meaning words are two-edged swords. If you saw a little baby toddling about with an open knife in his little hands, you would spring with alarm to take it away. Here is a soul in blindness and darkness carrying a sharp sword of destruction for its own ruin.

Beware of double-meaning words against purity ; they are worse in some respects than more vulgar and coarse ones, for the last disgust and repel us, while the former make a deep impression on the mind by their wit, and rankle in the heart, infecting it with filthy and unclean ideas.

Show your displeasure plainly as soon as you perceive that another is aiming to insinuate anything improper under the cover of a double-meaning word. Sometimes a dead silence will be the best rebuke, or a sudden deafness may seize you. If the thing is repeated, you may show your displeasure more decidedly. There is generally some shame and sense of decency even in the most hardened; and if such attempts are put down in the outset, it may prevent a great deal of trouble and sin afterwards, and be the means of making such people more careful how they expose their own vulgar and coarse minds to public gaze. The wicked are and must be abashed in the presence of virtue and purity.

Keep, then, a guard on your eyes, your ears, your mouth, your hands, and all your senses, that you may be far from any occasion to sin against this holy virtue; and God will give you great graces.

Remember the admirable answer once made by a king. King Roger kept his eyes under such complete control that, although constantly meeting people, for the space of three years it was observed that he never looked a woman in the face. A person who had observed this asked him the reason, and got this reply: " When a man does what he can, and avoids the occasion of sin, then God on his part does what He can, and preserves him from sin ; but when a man rashly throws himself in the way of danger, then he is justly deserted by God, and permitted to fall into sin.''

CHAPTER LXVII.

OF MODESTY IN DRESS.

THERE is an old maxim, that ''fine feathers make fine birds,'' and this maxim is always applied with contempt to overdressed women. The meaning seems to be about this: She has got a fine rig on her back, but very little sense in her head ; she prides herself on her fine dress, but there is little else to be proud of.

Modesty and simplicity in dress are great ornaments to a woman, and the woman whose heart is bent on serving God and gaining Heaven must and will show this modesty and simplicity in her attire? Why? Simply because her soul is taken up with something more important than dress. She remembers that she has been placed here on earth, an immortal soul, to accomplish her destiny by serving and loving God, and not like a wax figure in a shop-window, to be a machine to hang finery on.

Her rule is rather that of the Gospel: "Having food and raiment, let us be therewith content"; and she bears in mind the words of the Saviour of the world: "Be not solicitous for your life what you shall eat, nor for your body what you shall put on; the life is more than the food, and the body more than the raiment" (Matt. vi. 25).

Such was the idea of St. Frances of Rome. Of a noble and wealthy family, married to one of the most accomplished and prominent men, she was obliged, by her station, to wear rich and magnificent dresses, but it was always against her inclination. She would not act contrary to the wishes of her husband and his family, but she wore under her rich dress a habit of the coarsest and roughest material. At last the grace and favor of God to her was so openly manifested, that her husband told her that he would not stand in her way any longer, but that she should follow exactly what she deemed pleasing to God. For the rest of her life she never wore any other gown than one of coarse green cloth. This would not have been right ordinarily, for we must generally dress according to our stations in life and avoid every singularity; but her holiness had become so well known that it was proper in her case, and only gave edification to all who saw her.

So it was also with St. Elizabeth, who was

of a royal family. She took care to be dressed suitably and neatly, and was much admired for her simple and innocent grace of manner and dress; but still it was observed that she avoided every possible display of ornament and unnecessary extravagance, and seemed to be entirely free from all that vanity and lightness so common to rich and beautiful young ladies of her class. As soon as misfortune came upon her she gladly laid aside every vestige of her greatness, and clothed herself in the poorest and coarsest apparel.

And there are now many ladies of fortune and high position who, with the spirit of Catholic piety, while they strive to avoid singularity and remark, study to dress just as plainly and inexpensively as possible.

What a contrast here is to the giddy girl who earns by hard labor a few dollars a month, and lays it all out on her back!

You, maybe, have heard of the fable of the jackdaw and the peacock. The jackdaw stole some of the peacock's feathers and stuck them in his tail, and then went strutting about among the peacocks; but as soon as he opened his mouth to make a noise the cheat was discovered, and falling upon him they picked him bare on the spot.

So it is with these girls so fashionably rigged up : as soon as they open their mouths to speak, or as soon as you get a good look in their faces, you see at once how much out of place all this finery is.

CHAPTER LXVIII.

ADVANTAGES OF MODESTY IN DRESS.

I DO not mean to say that a good and pious working-girl should dress either shabbily or much out of the prevailing fashion. That would be a mistake of another kind, and would attract unpleasant observation upon her, and be disedifying. But I mean to say that she should study to dress neatly and modestly, and with economy ; laying out as little of her earnings as she can on dress ; avoiding expensive material, such as the wealthy can afford, and wearing that which becomes her better, and is at the same time far more suitable to her condition and her means.

A prudent girl will understand what I mean. She knows that while she does not spend more than a quarter as much as some others, she can dress quite as well ; nay, in better taste and keeping.

Now let me speak of the advantages which such a course will procure those who follow it. Of course, the spiritual benefit to their own souls is the chief and greatest ; but I do not wish to speak of that, as so much has already been said. It is also of very great advantage towards securing a happy and prosperous life here.

If a girl prefers to remain single, it will enable her to do a great deal of good ; and what purer source of happiness is there than that ?

It may be she has dear relations—father and mother, brothers and sisters—who need her help, and she, by her simplicity and economy in dress, can render them great assistance. What a delight it is to think of the happiness she has caused at home when she gets a letter filled with love and blessings from those who are so dear to her ! Is not this far purer and sweeter than if, with cold-blooded selfishness, she had loaded all her money on her own back, to parade the streets and make a show of herself?

If she has no needy relations who require her help, she has the opportunity of doing something to help the wretched and afflicted poor ; to feed the hungry and clothe the naked ; and to receive the Lord's benediction in return, the same as if it had been done for Himself, according to His assurance : "Inasmuch as ye have done it unto the least of these my brethren, you have done it unto me" (St. Matt. xxv. 40).

Our Lord Jesus Christ showed once to St. Zita, in a miraculous manner, that He never forgets this promise.

One Christmas Eve St. Zita was going out of

the house to attend the first Mass. It was very cold, and her master insisted on her wearing his own warm fur cloak. The first thing she saw when she got to church was a poor man, his teeth chattering with cold, and moaning bit· terly. She went up to him and asked him if she could do anything to help him. He pointed to her cloak, and instantly she took it off her own shoulders and gave it to him, telling him to give it back after Mass, and she would lead him to a warm fire. When Mass was over she looked for the poor man, but he was nowhere to be found, and she had to go home without her cloak.

Of course her master was very angry, and scolded her without measure. All day she bore it with patience until toward night, when a poor man appeared on the principal staircase of the house; his countenance had a look of so much benignity that every one who saw him was charmed. The fur cloak was in his hand; and, in the presence of her master, he returned it to St. Zita, thanking her for her charity.

As they were about to speak to him he vanished like a gleam of lightning, leaving in their hearts such joy and consolation that they had no doubt that it was our Lord Himself who had appeared to them.

There are many such examples in the lives of the saints, to show us that when in the spirit of faith we deny ourselves to relieve the poor, we receive the same blessing as if it had been the Lord Jesus Christ Himself who had come asking alms, and whom we had the happiness of relieving in His necessity.

If you do not relieve the poor, you may, in imitation of St. Mary Magdalen, anoint our Lord's feet with precious ointment. How can this be done? By contributing to the erecting and beautifying of churches and altars. The girls who live out have been called the church-builders, and it is a glorious title for them. Out of their hard earnings they have done so much for the glory and honor of God and for the salvation of immortal souls that God will never forget it.

King David exclaimed: "Dost thou see that I dwell in a house of cedar, and the ark of God is lodged within curtains?" (2 Kings vii. 2). And he gave his whole attention to provide for the erection of the Temple.

So what a heartfelt pleasure it must be to the pious girl to deny herself something in dress, in order that the Lord of Glory may have more suitable adornment in His House, where He dwells out of love to us! Surely it can be but little satisfaction to be bedizened out in the height of the fashion, and to see everything mean and unsuitable about the altar and tabernacle.

But maybe the good girl intends, in God's good time, to settle down in life as the head of a family. If her heart and soul are in dress,

what kind of a husband will she be likely to get?
I fear a very poor stick, as they say; some one
as giddy-pated and thoughtless as herself; probably some dissipated young man, who is taken
by mere outside show; for a more prudent and
steady young man would think a good deal before
he would make up his mind to take such a woman
for a wife.

He might be attracted at first, but he would
say to himself: "See here, before I go farther,
let us see what a marriage with such a girl as
this will be likely to bring me to. I can never
earn enough to keep her in clothes, let alone the
expenses of a family. Oh, no! she may be well
enough to flirt with a little while, but I mean to
look elsewhere for a wife."

Let us suppose, however, by unusual good fortune such a girl gets a good husband. Now they
start in life to maintain themselves and provide
for the future. Had she been saving, she might
have laid up a snug little sum that would have
given him a good start in business or trade. As
it is, he has nothing; and both of them are sadly
put back, live in discomfort, and very likely will
continue to do so the better part of their lives.

Many a girl who has made quite a show in
the way of fashionable dress, has settled down
into the most slovenly and dirty wife, and has
finally been glad enough to get the commonest
rags to cover her back.

CHAPTER LXIX.

OF MODESTY IN DRESS—CONTINUATION.

KEEP neat and take care of what you wear; make it last. What matter is it if your bonnet or your dress is a little out of fashion?

Study, then, simplicity and economy in your dress, for these things are suitable to your condition and station in life, and are pleasing to God. Avoid setting your heart on dress and fashion, for they will produce in your heart vanity and self-love, that destroy the love of God. Hear what the Holy Ghost says of such things: And the Lord said: "Because the daughters of Sion are haughty and have walked with outstretched necks and wanton glances of the eye, and made a noise as they walked with their feet, and moved in a set pace, the Lord will make bald the crown of the head of the daughters of Sion, and the Lord will discover their hair. In that day the Lord will take away the ornament of shoes, and little moons, and chains, and necklaces, and bracelets, and bonnets, and bodkins, and ornaments of the legs, and tablets, and sweet balls, and ear-rings and rings, and jewels hanging on the forehead, and changes of apparel, and short cloaks, and fine linen, and crisping-pins, and looking-glasses, and lawns, and head-bands, and fine veils. And instead of a sweet smell, there shall be stench ; and instead of a girdle, a cord ; and instead of curled hair, baldness; and instead of a stomacher, hair-cloth " (Isai. iii. 16–24).

Here it is not meant to condemn the use of each of these things separately, but to condemn most severely any inordinate and excessive following of worldly fashion.

So St. Paul says: " In like manner let women in decent apparel adorn themselves with modesty and sobriety, not with plaited hair, or gold, or pearls, or costly array. But as it becometh women professing piety with good works " (1 Tim. ii. 9).

And St. Peter: " Whose adorning, let it not be the outward plaiting of the hair, or the wearing of gold, or the putting on of apparel, but the hidden man of the heart, in the incorruptibility of a quiet and meek spirit, which is rich in the sight of the Lord " (1 St. Pet. iii. 3, 4).

And in another place the Holy Ghost says: " Glory not in apparel at any time" (Eccles. xi. 4). St. John Chrysostom says on this subject: " The dancer, the prostitute, and the actor wear more handsome and costly habiliments than you. Besides, you glory in a thing of the pleasure of which the moth may deprive you ; you glory in a thing which worms produce and destroy. Buy a garment woven above, a garment admirable and splendid, made of true gold : this gold is not dug from the earth by convicts, it is the product of virtue. Let us be clothed in that robe which is wrought, not by mechanics and slaves, but by the Lord Himself."

Avoid everything tending in the least to im. modesty in your dress, no matter if it be the fashion. It is never the fashion for modest women who fear God; for such women never follow evil fashions. St. Chrysostom says of those who do so : "They make a sport of the death of souls, merely to gratify a senseless pride, a pitiful vanity. They adhere to sin a thousand times more by the indecency of their apparel than by the voice."

Low-necked dresses and bare arms give an air of vulgarity to those who wear them, and provoke much remark which would cause the blush of shame to crimson the cheek of the modest. They cause mortal sin sometimes, more even than a more open and undisguised indecency, which would disgust by its coarseness.

Consult, then, the Holy Ghost, listen to His voice in your hearts, and rather be too particular than careless in so important a matter.

To conclude, and to show you the difference between the pomp and splendor of the world and true Christian simplicity, let me give you the account of the journey of Melania, a noble Ro-

man lady, to visit St. Paulinus at Nola. I will
relate it in the very words of St. Paulinus himself. But first I must tell you who Melania was.
She was a noble Roman matron, possessed of
immense riches, which were left at her disposal
at the death of her husband, which occurred
when she was only twenty-three years old.
From that time she determined to devote herself
to the service of God entirely, and she spent
many years in the Holy Land, having sold her
property and distributed it freely for the relief
of the needy. At the end of these years she
came back to Rome for a short time, to encourage her only son and her granddaughter to devote themselves also entirely to Christ. It was
on this occasion that she, her daughter-in-law,
and granddaughter, made this pious visit to St.
Paulinus. Now for the account.

"She hastened," said he, "to come and visit
us, accompanied by her children in all their
pomp and show. We saw the triumph of the
glory of the Lord in the different style and equi-
page with which the mother and her daughters
(Albina and the young Melania) made the same
journey. Their mother was seated on a poor, lean
horse, more worthless and meaner than an ass,
but she was followed by proud senators, who
walked surrounded by all the pomp which the
grandeur of their position and their opulence
could afford. The Appian Way was not only

covered, but completely crowded and resplendent, with pavilioned cars and gilded carriages, drawn by horses superbly harnessed, and a very great number of chariots; but the beauty of Christian humility far outshone all this vain display.

"While the rich admired her who, though poor, was holy, she despised their wealth. We there were witnesses in this humiliation of the proud world to that which God esteems, since we behold royal purple, and silk, and robes embroidered with gold, humble themselves before the black and worn garments of serge.

"We blessed the Lord, Who makes the humble wise, and in Whose sight true humility is a sure exaltation; Who filleth with good things and satiates with His holy viands those who hunger and thirst after His grace and justice, leaving the rich in their want."

CHAPTER LXX.

ON TRUTHFULNESS.

THE prophet David cries out, in the 30th Psalm, "Into thy hands I commend my soul, because thou hast redeemed me, O Lord, thou God of truth" (Ps. xxx. 6). What confidence and childlike reliance on God is here, and what does it rest upon? On the truth of the Almighty: "Heaven and earth shall pass away, but my word shall not pass away" (St. Matt. v. 18). He is the eternal truth, and all our hopes and all our happiness depend on it that he is so.

So we say: "O my Lord! I believe, because Thou art the infallible truth." Truth, then, and perfect truth in God, ought to be most dear to us. We should say frequently: How lovely is the truth of God. Thanks be to God that He is the perfect truth. The God of perfect truth, who cannot deceive in the smallest particular, has redeemed me; praise be to His holy Name!

If this perfect truth and sincerity of God is the foundation of all our hopes in Him, a perfect truth and sincerity on our part ought to correspond to it. Jesus Christ is the pattern.

and we must be the copy. As St. Paul says :
We must put off the old man, "who is corrupt-
ed according to the desires of error ; and put on
the new man, who, according to God, is created
in justice and holiness of truth. Wherefore,
putting away lying, speak ye the truth every
man with his neighbor" (Eph. iv. 22-25). The
soul that desires to make her salvation sure
will begin by holding all lying in abomination.
The lying tongue, says Scripture, is an abomination to the Lord, and so it should be to her.
And she should make a thorough work of it,
casting out all lies, small or great, and speaking
the truth in all things.

Some may imagine that it is enough to be
careful and speak the truth in all matters of
importance. It is not enough. We must speak
truth in small and great, in all things. And I
will tell you the reason why. Sincerity is the
basis and foundation of the Christian character,
and lying and falsehood are directly opposed to
this sincerity. Now, a real sincerity of character will throw out all exceptions ; it will and
must extend to all things. Just as the magnet
draws to itself all the little bits of iron in its
neighborhood, so will true sincerity of character
draw all our little actions and words to itself
and make them all sincere and truthful.

You can all understand how if God could lie
to us in any matter, however small, all our con-

fidence in Him would be destroyed. In the same way if we find a person lying in small matters, we conclude there is no real and true sincerity of character there.

The habit of lying in little things will bring on the habit of lying in great ones, for lying is a weakness and cowardice, a want of Christian courage, that basely and meanly gives up pleasing Jesus Christ for fear of some man or woman who may be displeased. When this road is once entered upon it is travelled over very rapidly. You have given up to this cowardly fear in a little matter. You are more cowardly now than before and more ready to give up again. A greater thing comes up ; you are afraid to tell the truth, and lie again. So a little lie draws on a big one, and that another, until a habit of lying is formed, and God only knows whether it will ever be broken up.

The worst of it is that this lying eats out and corrupts the whole character ; it extends to all kinds of things ; as well to God as to man. If you deceive your neighbor, you will become deceitful and double-dealing in all your ways. You will begin to deceive yourself, and frame excuses for sin, and plaster it over until your own conscience is blinded by a false light.

And maybe this deceit and falsehood may corrupt and infect your heart to such an extent that your penance may be false also, and bring you to the bar of God unforgiven, when it is too late to repair the evil. '

Do not say, then, that any lie whatever is a small thing. It is the devil that prompts us to utter such maxims. He wants to throw a small cord around us, in order to bind us by and by with a strong and heavy chain.

CHAPTER LXXI.

SCRIPTURE ON LYING.

IT is in view of this nature of lying and these consequences which are so apt to follow, when it is allowed to go on in little things, that God so strongly denounces lying in the Scriptures.

Lies are set down as coming all from the devil. "When the devil speaketh a lie he speaketh of his own, for he is a liar, and the father of lies" (St. John viii. 44). This shows in what detestation God holds lies. The devil is his great enemy, and lies are from the devil. "God hateth a lying tongue" (Prov. vi. .17). "Lying lips are an abomination to the Lord" (Prov. xii. 22). Lying is said to be a chief characteristic of the wicked. "The wicked are estranged and go astray speaking lies" (Ps. lviii. 3). "They delight in lies and curse inwardly"' (Ps. lxii. 4).

Now listen to the threats of God against lying. "He that speaketh lies shall not escape" (Prov. xiv. 5). "The mouth that speaketh lies shall be stopped" (Ps. lxiii. 11). "But a lying tongue is but for a moment" (Prov. xii. 19). And, finally: "All liars shall have their portion in the lake that burns with brimstone and fire" (Apoc. xxi. 8). I could quote many others to the same effect, for there is no vice in the whole Scripture held up with such loathing and scorn.

The good and holy have always had a great dread of this vice. So Job, that model of Christian perfection, exclaims: "As long as breath remaineth in me, and the Spirit of God in my nostrils, my lips shall not speak iniquity, neither shall my tongue contrive lying" (Job xxvii. 2). Get this text of Holy Scripture by heart, and often pass it through your mind and often repeat it with your lips, that your heart may be as entirely set against all lying as Job's was. God will reward such a disposition with his richest graces.

A beautiful example is recorded of a holy bishop named Anthimus. He was willing to lay down his life rather than tell what many folks would be ready to call a small lie. It happened in this way. The emperor sent out

his soldiers to seize him and lead him away to
death. They came to his house and found him
at home. He received them with so much kindness, and entertained them so hospitably, that
he completely won their hearts, so that they
rose up to go, saying: "We will tell the emperor we came here but could not find you."
"No," says he, "you will tell him no such
thing. It is not right for a Christian to lie."
He made himself ready, accompanied them before the emperor, and met his death by the
stroke of the sword.

That is the true love of Jesus Christ, not to
say, Lord, Lord, I love Thee, and go on lying,
but to be willing to suffer loss or reproaches, as
this good bishop did, being ready to lay down
his life rather than utter the smallest lie.

Great rewards are promised for such holy dispositions. Hear what St. John says of the one
hundred and forty-four thousand who follow
the Lamb whithersoever he goeth: "These
are purchased from among men, the first-fruits
to God and to the Lamb: and in their mouth
was found no lie: for they are without spot before the throne of God" (Apoc. xiv. 4, 5).

Keep in mind, then, always this exhortation
of the holy Apostle St. Paul to all Christians:
"Lie not one to another; stripping yourself of
the old man with his deeds, and putting on the
new, him who is renewed unto knowledge, ac-

cording to the image of Him who created him."
And pray, with King Solomon: "Two things I
have asked of Thee, O Lord, do not deny me:
let vanity and lying lips be far from me."

CHAPTER LXXII.

THE DEVIL'S PRETEXTS FOR LYING.

THE devil is the father of lies, the parent of a
numerous progeny of lies, which he stirs
up in the hearts of those who give ear to him,
and all the various pretexts and excuses which
he insinuates, to hinder them from telling the
truth. Now, as I have already told you of the
malignant and poisonous character of lying, I
must so lay bare all the roots of it, all the pretexts and excuses for it, that you be on your
guard against them, and destroy the very root
of the matter.

Just as the doctor, when he has a cancer to
cure, takes good care to cut out every root of it,
and searches and probes down deep to find
them, for fear, if any should remain undiscov-
ered and alive under the flesh, the cancer might
again gather strength and be worse than before.

The first of these excuses arises from the desire to get rid of some pain or punishment we
have deserved, most generally of a reprimand or

scolding. A girl has been negligent of her duty. Her mistress goes down into the kitchen and finds a great heap of dirty dishes that ought to have been washed and put away long ago ; or the floor that she directed to be scrubbed is in a filthy condition, while the girl has had abundance of time to do it ; or the beds are not made up, late in the day ; or the meals are behind time, or half-cooked or burned, or many other things neglected which I cannot specify.

Now, instead of an acknowledgment and a resolve to do better, there are a lot of lies ready for the occasion. She had such and such things to do and was overburdened with work, or she felt very unwell, or the fire would not kindle, or the stove would not draw, or she had to go after this or that ; anything for an excuse.

The mistress may be deceived sometimes, but she at last finds out that these excuses are a pack of lies, and the result is, more ill-temper and vexation and scolding, and dismissal, than if all had been frankly and sincerely owned and amended.

"I have found her careless and lazy, but she has one merit, she does speak the truth," is what the lady of the house will say of a truthful girl, and this speaking the truth will atone for many a shortcoming.

Sometimes the lying is to cover up some injury to the property of your employer. You have broken dishes, or allowed something to go to ruin through carelessness. You think something may be deducted from your wages, or that you will be scolded, and you deny it. Have you not deserved all this? Of course. Well, then, if you will not commit a double sin, own up and take the consequences like a Christian, and not behave as a cowardly heathen would.

"Oh! but," says the father of lies, "it was but a small matter; what is the use of having a fuss about it? I know she will scold hard if she knows it." Say: "Get behind me, Satan; I will own up, and bring to naught all your tricks."

Let me tell you what happened once from telling a lie about these small matters. The Empress Eudoxia received the gift of a perfect and beautiful apple from her husband, the emperor. She sent it as a present to a sick nobleman called Paulinus. The emperor by chance found out that Paulinus had this apple, and being of a jealous disposition, he asked his wife what she had done with the apple he gave her. She, out of a cowardly fear of a little displeasure, instead of owning that she had given it away, said that she had eaten it. Her reply fixed the evil suspicion so deep in the emperor's mind that Paulinus was ordered to be slain, and the empress was divorced and sent away into banishment. So much for a lie about an apple.

Sometimes the lie is to conceal a petty dishonesty. You have taken some trifling thing for your own use, or given it away to your friends. You perceive that a sincere avowal and acknowledgment of this fault will not injure your character, or make you less esteemed, but the idea of shame puts you up to deny it, and tell many lies to screen yourself. How much better to come out at once with the truth, and ask forgiveness, being determined to be more particular in future. The shame you experience will be a powerful means to keep you from ever falling into the like fault again. You lie about these things, and when it comes to more important things in Confession the devil is all ready to suggest other lies. In the first place, the whole truth is not told ; very likely the value is concealed, the thing is made light of, for shame or for fear of being made to restore, and a lie is told to Almighty God.

St. Peter said to Ananias and Saphira, his wife, You have not lied to man, but to God, and by God's judgment, for our warning, they fell dead on the spot. How many lies are not told to God in the same way. Ananias brought the price of his field that he had sold and laid it at the Apostle's feet. But it was not the whole **price, as he pretended and said it was.**

So the girl comes to Confession and lays down her sin at the priest's feet, but not the whole sin. There is a lie in that Confession. She is so in the habit of lying that she can't tell a straight story even in Confession. Ananias had an excuse for his lie which this girl has not.

His money was his own and he was not obliged to bring one cent of it to St. Peter. St. Peter said to him: "Whilst the field remained, did it not remain to thee? and being sold, was it not in thy power?" (Acts v. 4). He told what people would call a simple lie, that injured no one. He, out of vanity, wanted to get credit for what he did not deserve; yet he heard these fearful words: "Why has Satan tempted thy heart to lie to the Holy Ghost?" This most fearful example of God's judgment on lying was no doubt given as a special warning that lying in general is an evil thing, and especially when it comes to dealing with God in the tribunal of penance.

Another troop of lies arises from a desire to screen others. "I would not care so much for myself, but it is a good thing to get her off, or him." No, let him or her manage their own affairs, but keep your soul clear of lying for them. To screen a friend may be well enough, if it can be done without sin. But you have no right to sin that good may come.

This is the devil's artifice to cheat souls. He holds out something which appears good, and says it is no harm to do so and so: "Don't you see what good you will do by it: the good is a great deal more than all the sin. Don't be so dreadfully scrupulous: the world could not get on at all if folks acted on such principles." Say, again: "Get behind me, Satan; I will have none of your tricks."

CHAPTER LXXIII.

EXAMPLES OF TRUTHFULNESS.

A BISHOP, called Firmus—that is, firm, but, as St. Augustine says, more firm in his will to keep God's holy commandments—when the emperor's bailiffs came to him, inquiring for a man whom the bishop had hidden, replied that he would neither betray the man to them nor tell them any lie. They being pagans, tortured him severely and led him away to the emperor, but the bishop's sincerity and goodness made such an impression that the emperor, without any hesitation, pardoned the culprit at the bishop's request.

Tell no lie under any pretext of good, or appearance of humility, or of any other virtue. A venerable hermit, St. John of Egypt, was visited by a company of good men who desired to receive his holy instructions. He received them most kindly, and they begged his blessing. But he replied : '' Is there no one among you in Holy Orders ?'' They answered, "No." The saint then looked at each one in turn attentively until he came to the youngest, when he pointed his finger at him and said : '' This one is a deacon.'' Now, this was really a deacon, but he had concealed the fact from a desire to avoid being honored by men whom he considered so much superior to himself in point of holiness. And out of this motive he denied it again. Now notice the conduct of St. John. He took the hand of the young man, kissed it to show his respect for his office, and addressed him in these words : '' Take care, my son, how you disavow the grace you have received from God, for fear a good thing may not cause you to fall into evil, and humility plunge you in lying ; for we must never lie, neither out of a bad motive, nor out of a good one ; for a lie does not come from God, but from the author of evil, as our Saviour has taught us.'' An admirable instruction which you should never forget.

A little boy of nine years of age gives us one equally good. This little boy had forgotten something his father had commanded him to do, and fearing a whipping, he began, as boys do, to cry. The servants asked him the reason, and made up a plausible lie for him to tell to clear himself before his father. "Oh !" said they, "just say so and so, and you will get off; but if you tell the truth you will surely be well flogged." The boy replied : " It is better to be killed than to lie : let my father do what he likes ; for my part, if I die I will tell no lie ; how could I dare to appear before the Blessed Virgin after I had told an untruth !"

Suppose, then, that you do succeed by these lies in escaping a scolding or a punishment, what does that signify ? You have a guilty conscience. How can you appear with confidence before God in prayer ? How can you ask the intercession of the Blessed Virgin or the saints who were such haters of all lying.

You have saved your own interest, or your feelings, but have inflicted a great dishonor on God and a shame on His holy religion. "That's a Catholic." " That's one that goes to Confession, but she don't scruple to tell a lie when she finds it convenient." " Oh ! she is very religious, but you can't believe a word she says." " There is one thing about Catholic girls, they will lie "; and a host more of such expressions fly about. They are often unjust, but still I fear there is but too often truth in them.

We may say it is very unjust to attack the church for the sins of her members ; but let the members bear in mind that such things will be said if they give occasion by their sins.

In conclusion, then, be determined—out of the fear, and, much more, for the love of God ; out of regard to our own souls, and for the honor of the church of Christ, and the good of other souls who see in you an example—" to put away the old man with his corruptions, and put on the new man who is in sincerity and truth " ; and " avoiding all lying," resolve " to speak the truth every man to his neighbor " (Eph. iv. 22-24).

CHAPTER LXXIV.

WHETHER TO MARRY OR NOT.

WE now approach a subject of the highest importance to the greater part of our working-girls, namely : that which relates to marriage, by which they attain a settlement for life.

I suppose almost every girl gives this matter a good deal of attention, as her future well-being depends so much upon it, and therefore I think it worth while to say something in respect to the way she ought to look upon it, and behave herself in regard to it.

Marriage is a state of life instituted by God

Himself, for the welfare, happiness, and continuance of the human family. He has implanted in the heart, therefore, a desire for it, which induces the greater part of mankind on arriving at mature age to enter into it. Young men and young women seek for a congenial and suitable companion with whom they can spend their lives in comfort and happiness.

This state of life affords a young woman a permanent home of her own, in which she has a husband and children to love and care for. We must all have some one to love, and although it is true that the love of God is sufficient to fill the heart, and to fill it completely, yet God has willed that ordinarily the love of kindred should also solace us and make life more endurable.

Now, our parents, brothers and sisters, or more distant relations, do not supply that love which the heart craves. They either pass away from this world and leave us behind, or are taken up with their own affairs and do not love us sufficiently, so that when God does not call to a single life, a nearer tie and stronger love is required, which marriage can alone afford. God has said : '' Wherefore a man shall leave father and mother, and cleave unto his wife, and they shall be two in one flesh '' (Gen. ii. 24).

I am not surprised, then, that a girl should wish to settle herself in life by marriage. She may be happy enough, and well enough off, at the present, but she has to consider the future; her life in middle age and when she is old.

She may very well have a repugnance to being left alone in the world as she advances in life, and shudders at the dreary prospect. Or she may have a proper ambition to be her own mistress, the head of her own household, instead of remaining all her days at some kind of service in an inferior position.

Reflections of this kind naturally present themselves to her mind and induce a conclusion that if she finds a good opportunity she will get married, and I am sure I see no impropriety in such a determination.

Still, she should remember that there is an ''if'' about it, and the matter does not lie in her own power. She may never find the opportunity to make a suitable match, and if she does not, it is a clear indication of God's will that she should not marry, notwithstanding she may wish it.

Remember the old saying: ''Matches are made in Heaven.'' If you are to marry, God will provide a suitable match at the right time; and if He does not, you are to remain content with His holy will.

From this I draw the conclusion that it is best for young women not to think too much on this subject, particularly when they are not receiving attentions which seem to point to an offer of marriage.

I do not see what good can come of it, and, on the contrary, a deal of harm. Thinking about it and talking of it will not bring it about any sooner. As soon as any anxiety to marry is perceived in a young woman, it produces a feeling of disgust in all who perceive it, and women who are supposed to be on the look-out for a match are commonly avoided. A natural modesty and reserve are far more attractive.

Again, you may become unhappy and discontented by dwelling on such thoughts. You become by them dissatisfied with God's providence concerning you, and a murmurer against Him, and entirely lose your tranquillity of mind, without which you cannot make progress in holiness and God's love.

But there is far greater danger—the danger of losing your innocence and purity of soul. The devil is ready to mix with what is proper and right that which is unfit and sinful. By dwelling anxiously on this matter of marriage and thinking too much about it, you expose yourself to very great danger of falling into sin.

My advice then is, that without thinking much about it, you commit the whole matter to God, begging Him to take care of you, and provide for your future life as shall seem most fitting in His eyes.

CHAPTER LXXV.

CONTINUATION.

BUT, on the other hand, there may be girls who are disinclined to marry. They find themselves very well contented in the single life, and do not wish to change their condition. They dread the cares and responsibility which they know to follow from the state of marriage, and choose to retain their freedom.

Some may be influenced principally by considerations of piety. They see in the single life greater opportunities to serve God than they think they would find in a married one. They fear that they will be too much taken up by the cares of a family and not be so much at liberty to devote themselves to piety and religion.

As St. Paul says: "And the unmarried woman and the virgin thinketh on the things of the Lord, that she may be holy both in body and spirit; but she that is married thinketh on the things of the world, how she may please her husband" (1 Cor.)

They bear in mind the examples of the Blessed Virgin and of so many of the saints who have consecrated themselves to God in holy vir-

ginity, and feel inclined to follow in their foot-
steps.

Now, I would advise these not to be too
hasty in making a decision, and above all to
avoid anything like a rash vow or promise to
God in reference to it.

There is plenty of time and no need of haste.
Notwithstanding such feelings, you may not
know your own mind or the will of God, and
there is no need of entangling yourself by any
rash proceeding.

I have known many, who seemed fully determined to remain single, who, on getting a
good offer, have changed their minds and accepted it. If they had in a moment of fervor
made any rash vow or promise on the subject
it would have been a serious detriment to them,
and, perhaps, been a subject of regret all their
lives.

And, sometimes, God's holy will may be different from what it seems to us at first sight.
We have an instance of this in the case of St.
Frances of Rome. She had a very strong desire
to live the life of a nun, but her father wished
her to marry and promised her to a nobleman of
the city. She shed many bitter tears, but on
praying earnestly and consulting pious and holy
advisers, she became fully convinced it was
God's will for her to marry. She did so, and in
this state of life she became a great saint.

Whether, then, you feel on the whole inclined to marry, or to remain single, keep perfectly tranquil, and do not let your mind dwell
much on the subject, being ready to follow God's
will when He shows it to you more clearly by
sending you an opportunity of marriage.

Then you can consider more particularly
whether you should avail yourself of it or
not.

In making up your mind you can consider,
first, your own circumstances : how you feel inclined ; your habits ; your disposition, and other
things which ought to be considered in your
case ; secondly, the character of the other party :
his moral character, his disposition and temper,
his ability to maintain you ; in short, whether
you will find it for your spiritual and temporal
advantage to take him for a husband or not.
Pray to God to direct you with an earnest desire
to follow His will. After this, decide reason-
ably and quietly what you conceive to be best,
and afterwards do not allow yourself to be
troubled, for you have followed the will of God
in regard to you, and could not do better than
that.

In general, you are the one who will have to
make a decision for yourself, as you know yourself and your own circumstances better than anybody else can know them ; but it may be you
have a prudent friend who knows you well, and

whose advice may be of assistance to you ; in that case it would be well to ask advice.

You know the maxim, No man can judge in his own case. If you suspect passion is running away with you, and blinding you to your real interest, the judgment of a sincere friend, who will not flatter, may be of the utmost importance to you.

Now, let us suppose you are one of those who do not intend to marry, who have pretty much made up your mind to put away all advances on the subject ; you ought to regulate your manners accordingly. There ought to be a special reserve and modesty about you. To invite attention, to run about freely in the company of young men, to joke and banter—in short, to act as if you had no such determination—is to sail under false colors. It is to hold out expectations that you do not intend to fulfil. Let there be, then, a correspondence between your interior disposition and your external manners, that you may not lead others astray and yourself into a grievous snare.

CHAPTER LXXVI.

GREAT NEED OF PRUDENCE.

ON our coast, which is so stormy and dangerous, there are many safe harbors where the
mariner feels secure against the violence of every
storm.   But when he approaches these harbors
he is wide awake and pays the closest attention
to every movement of his vessel ; and good reason he has for it too.   Here is a shoal on this
side, there is a ledge of rocks on the other ; here
the channel takes a short turn ; at no time of his
whole voyage is there so much danger of ship-
wreck as now.   He must not relax his vigilance
an instant until he drops anchor in the very
spot where he will remain.

So it is when about to anchor one's self for
life in the state of matrimony.   The whole approach to this state is filled with the greatest
danger, and requires untiring vigilance to get
through it safely without a wreck of happiness
in this world and the next.

And this danger is greater, it seems to me, in
this country and at this time than at any other.
Why ?   Because in other countries the inter-
course between young people is more restrained
and guarded than it can be here.   It is there

settled by custom that they shall not visit so often, or be so much together as is the case here. The parents or friends have far more to say and to arrange there, while here more depends on the parties themselves. Many a girl has no father or mother to look out for her and advise her. She has to manage everything for herself the best she can. On all these accounts far more discretion and prudence is required on the part of a young woman in this country than anywhere else.

There is a peculiar modesty and shyness which springs up in the heart when one changes from the state of childhood to that of womanhood. No doubt God has given this to be a safeguard at the most dangerous period of life. When one could, as a light-hearted, innocent girl, speak and act with freedom, she must, as a young woman, keep an eye upon all her actions, that nothing may go beyond the bounds of propriety and be a snare to herself or to others.

Many women of this age moving about in the world are forming acquaintances and intimacies more or less close, and their entire future depends upon what they are.

Let us lay down, then, a few rules of prudence as to how she should conduct herself in that dangerous period of life which extends from the time of her arriving at mature age until she is married.

Let us see what intimacies it would be prudent for her to form, and how she should behave herself during the period of the courtship.

CHAPTER LXXVII.

WHAT INTIMACIES TO FORM.

BE careful what acquaintances you make. There are many young men of pleasing appearance, but who are demons in heart. Keep a guard, then, that you do not allow your feelings to get too much interested before you have time to make some kind of a judgment whether to allow an intimacy to be formed.

If you discover a heart filled with bad and impious principles, one that is a proud scoffer at religion or seems destitute of religious principles, *i. e.*, an infidel, whether he goes by the name of Catholic or not, avoid such a one.

There are plenty of such, real infidels at heart. They smooth it over when they want to marry some Catholic girl, who would be shocked at a plain open avowal of their sentiments, and when the marriage is over they conceal it no longer, but take delight in ridiculing religion ; in destroying the faith and love of their wives ; and if they have families, in ruining their immortal souls.

Now, these girls who marry such men, and who pay for it by the bitterest tears, perhaps for their whole lifetime, had they only exercised the slightest prudence, had they prayed to God and not been blinded by their own silly and unreasonable passion, would have noticed enough in their manners and conversation to have put them on their guard, and they would have sooner cut off their right hand than to have united their fate for life and death with them.

Says St. Paul: "Bear not the yoke together with unbelievers. For what participation hath justice with injustice? Or what fellowship hath light with darkness? And what agreement hath Christ with Belial?"—*i. e.*, the devil.

Again: If you discover a want of moral principle, that the person is the slave of any grievous sin, be on your guard, think not to take such a person as your partner for life. If the young man drinks freely and gets intoxicated, and there is a real danger that he will turn out a drunkard, for God's sake, and your own soul's, form no intimacy with such a one. What are you going to marry for? A quiet, peaceful home, and the opportunity of furthering your salvation.

The drunkard's home you well know is a picture of hell on earth, with its everlasting strife, disorder, burning passions, and hatred.

Is that the school in which you expect to learn the way of salvation?

I speak of this sin of drunkenness because it is the bitter root from which all kinds of vices and horrors may be expected to grow. There is no need of giving examples.

If you live in the city, go into the next street, or if in the country, go a short distance in your neighborhood, and you can find examples enough. Who is that bloated, coarse-looking woman who has not, apparently, combed her hair for a week, with a lot of ragged children bawling and fighting and cursing around her in her miserable, dirty hovel? That was, a few years ago, a pretty, modest girl, who was innocent and light-hearted, earning an easy living in a quiet, pleasant family, and attending to her duties regularly and with great delight to her soul.

She has not been to Mass for nearly a year, and cannot go, she says, "because her husband puts her about so." She wishes she was dead and gone, for her life is a burden to her.

And it was all her own fault. She knew enough about him when he was paying her attentions to put her on her guard. When he came to see her she smelled liquor in his breath repeatedly. Sometimes he showed quite plainly that he was under its influence, but she shut her eyes. "Oh!" she said, "I don't believe it is as bad as it looks.'' She did believe it, however, but she would not acknowledge it, for she had made up her mind to marry him.

Then friends came to warn her: '' Don't you know that young man is a drunkard? It is quite certain, and everybody knows it. You will rue the day you take him for a husband.'' She got obstinate, forgot God and even her own plain good sense and reason, and was determined to take him at any rate, even if she should lose her soul in consequence.

Ah, poor woman! I am afraid it will come to that, for your life is sinful, and there is little probability of its ever being changed for the better. Such examples speak a loud warning to you to teach you to avoid the misery of marrying a drunkard.

In the same way, if you discover any other confirmed vice, such as dishonesty, or impurity, do not let your acquaintance run on to an intimacy; do not let yourself get entangled, or think for a moment of marriage with such a one.

CHAPTER LXXVIII.

OF MIXED MARRIAGES.

THE question may be asked whether a Catholic young woman should in any case marry a person who is of a false or heretical religion. Cases may occur in which a really good and conscientious girl gets an offer of marriage that seems in all respects a good one, with this one exception—that the person is not a Catholic, and she is embarrassed as to what she should do.

A difference of religion between husband and wife is no doubt a great source of unhappiness in the marriage state, and a great evil. The want of sympathy in that which is the nearest and dearest to the heart must be a painful drawback to the love they should cherish towards each other, even if it does not lead to positive disagreement. The difficulties likely to arise in regard to the education of the children are great even if the father does not interfere. His example cannot fail to influence their ideas and conduct, and to put an obstacle in their way. On all accounts it is exceedingly desirable that a Catholic wife should have a Catholic husband.

But it may happen that a Catholic young

woman may not have an opportunity to marry
in her own religion. She may never have an
offer of marriage from a Catholic who has the
character and qualities likely to insure her happiness, and of course she cannot marry any one
unless he has.

She receives an offer from a Protestant of
good character and disposition, who is agreeable
in all respects except his religion; should she
reject this offer?

This depends on circumstances. In the first
place, he is bound by the law of the church to
solemnly promise you the free exercise of your
religion, and that all the children of the marriage shall be brought up Catholics. If he refuses to make these arrangements, you are
bound to let him go. You should not entertain the matter a moment; for how can you
make a contract in which you give up a part of
your duty to God? You are bound to see that
your children are educated in the one true faith
—and there can be but one—and you have no
right to place them in circumstances which expose them to the risk of losing it.

Here is a case for showing your true Christian principles and courage. You may have to
sacrifice your inclination, or, in a degree, your
worldly prospects, but the martyrs of old laid
down even their lives cheerfully for Jesus
Christ's sake. Depend upon it, our Lord will

not overlook any sacrifice you make for Him, nor fail to reward you abundantly.

If the person is willing to make the promises, inquire further whether he is strongly and blindly attached to his religion, and prejudiced against yours. If you find that such is the case, do not trust his promises. They will not be kept. Misery and ruin will follow such a union.

Do not trust that he will be converted. The prospect of it is too remote to build upon. The chance is that you will give way in a cowardly spirit and act against your conscience, and that the children will follow his example rather than your own.

There are plenty of examples of unhappy mothers who have dragged out a miserable existence during their whole life because they could not control their children, whom they loved so much, or see any prospect of their eternal salvation. Far better remain single than marry with such a prospect before you.

But if you see a candid, reasonable disposition in the one who solicits your hand, without prejudice against your religion, or at least without unreasonable prejudice which the truth cannot remove, and all is right in other respects, I would not like to stand in your way.

Be well assured that you are not deceived in these respects, and take time enough to make a safe decision. Pray to God for guidance, and take advice, and then decide the matter as seems on the whole the best and the most prudent.

CHAPTER LXXIX.

BEHAVIOR DURING COURTSHIP.

NOW let us suppose an acquaintanc has been formed and has gone so far that the subject of marriage is seriously thought of, it becomes a question of grave importance what kind of conduct one ought to observe.

Visits are frequently received, and it is easy to perceive that an interest in one another has been awakened. The young man says to himself: '' That is a fine young woman; I like her much, and perhaps I could not do better than to ask her for a wife.'' And the young woman says : '' If he should propose, I am not sure it would not be the best thing I could do to accept him, as he really seems very amiable and suitable.''

That is all very well; but the devil will try and take his advantage, and mix up with what is holy and good his suggestions of evil. You are frequently in each other's company. It would be better if some one were present at the same time. And when young women can so arrange it, they ought to strive to have some discreet companion in the room.

For example, one living at home should prefer that her parents, if they are good, should be present, or a brother or sister, as it shuts the door on all danger of undue familiarity, and of many temptations which would creep in.

If away from home and other girls are in the house, it would be as well that they should be present during these visits.

But it will often happen that there is no suitable person who can be present, and you must receive these visits alone; be careful that the most exact modesty and propriety is observed.

Now is the time when you have need to recommend yourself frequently to God, with a sincere and entire intention to maintain perfect purity in thought and word and deed. There is danger that evil thoughts will insinuate themselves in your heart, but be more ready now to drive them out at once than ever before.

Fly to God immediately, and say : "My God, my God, preserve me. I desire with my whole heart to remain in Thy love, and by Thy grace I am determined that I will."

It would seem to the world impossible to maintain purity at such a time ; but it is not impossible, indeed it is easy if you really desire to love God and are constant to beg his grace. Just as it was easy for God to shut the lion's mouth when Daniel was cast into their den, so that they could do him no harm, while he remained there with as much peace and tranquillity of soul as if in his own retired chamber.

It will be half the battle, as they say, if you are determined at the very outset to keep clear of every sin, and this determination will prepare you for every temptation that you may encounter.

If the young man is truly and sincerely pious, and has sentiments of the same kind, there will not be much difficulty. You have need of prayer and watchfulness, of course, as the devil is always on the lookout to ruin even the best and holiest souls ; but with these, I may say, there is no danger.

Do not allow visits, however, to be protracted to a late hour of the night. When the family retire to rest, let that be the signal for you also to do the same. Say at once, It is time to close this evening's visit, and to shut up the house. This may be done in a playful, cheerful manner, that will give no offence, and will cut off at once a world of difficulty. If the family keep very late hours themselves, then appoint a reasonable hour of your own, and when it arrives say in the same way, that it is time to retire, and bid good-night. Or say, that it is a rule with you not to allow a visit later than such an hour, for you need the time, in justice to God and to your employer. To sit up late defrauds God of his prayer, and renders you unfit for your duty the next day. This late visiting has been the devil's means of ruining thousands on thousands of well-disposed, good young women. The slightest reflection will cause you to see the evil of it yourself.

Now, let us suppose the young man who visits you is not one of a thousand, so pious and well-disposed, but less impressed with the idea of keeping a good and pure conscience, following passion sometimes, even though grievously offending God. Now what may very likely happen?

In the course of conversation some words of double meaning, some insinuations which are not exactly proper, covered up, it may be, under the idea of marriage, or under the cloak of affection. How does it become you to meet them? With great prudence.

If very slight, treat them as if you were entirely unconscious of them, and speak of something else, that you may show that you feel above taking any sort of notice of such things.

If the things said are too plain to be passed by, show yourself offended at once; say you are surprised at such talk, and never wish it to be repeated again.

By a decided conduct you may, once and for all, put a stop to everything of the sort, and make him see the evil of his conduct. Even a very bold and bad man is cowed down and made ashamed by a woman of real, heartfelt modesty.

Alas ! many young women do not act with this reserve. Some improper remark is made, and they laugh and show themselves pleased, perhaps make an equally improper reply, and the matter goes on now without much regard for God or care for sin. The heart is infected, and though prudence and fear of shame may restrain from certain shameful crimes, grievous sins are committed without number, the purity of the soul is gone, and the flame of hell is lighted up, which must be quenched by a bitter repentance, if ever quenched at all. Kissing and immodest freedom follow unchaste words, and in many cases ruin and disgrace and crime of the deepest character follow along after that. No one can tell what may be the final result of such a beginning.

CHAPTER LXXX.

CONTINUATION.

BUT, says some one : "A young man came to see me and kissed me, and used some familiarity toward me—it was not very bad." Why did you permit it? "I like him very well, and did not wish to offend him." Has it occasioned you any wilful evil thoughts? "I don't know exactly; I think not."

What a deadness of conscience here is! If such things have repeatedly happened, as is often the case, we may be quite sure there is sin, and abundance of wilful evil thoughts. The devil has deceived such a one. I am quite sure there cannot be a real peace of conscience under such circumstances. You may cry, "Peace! peace!" to yourself, "but there is no peace."

"But the young man whom I love will be displeased if I stop such familiarities: he will leave off visiting me, and I shall lose my opportunity of marrying one that I like."

Do not be so certain of that. No matter how vicious a man may be, he does not like to have an immodest woman for a wife. A man courts a young woman with the idea of marrying her; as the acquaintance goes on he begins to love her—now he has an idea it is a great thing to steal a kiss, as he says. He attempts with some roughness and freedom, and finds a lack of womanly modesty in the way it is received; that she is as willing to be kissed as he is to steal the kiss. Now, what is the result. He says: "By George! that girl is a little bit too free to please me. It is agreeable enough to go see her, to amuse myself and pass away the time, but I rather think I will look elsewhere for a wife. I want my wife to be of another sort." Some have even gone so far that they have determined to do their utmost to tempt and try any one they had an idea of marrying, being willing enough to commit sin, but determined never to marry any one who was not virtuous enough to resist their wicked attempts.

But suppose the time of courtship has been spent in this sinful way, and yet all goes on and marriage takes place; what then? The foundation of a jealous and unhappy married life has been laid during this courtship to bring forth its bitter fruits.

The wife may be quite innocent, but the husband is suspicious. "Oh! I know," he says, "how she behaved when I was courting her; if she could sin so easily then, why not now? I have not that confidence I should have had had she showed herself more discreet and prudent at that time."

This suspicion may arise from anything really immodest, though it may not have gone very far, for the virtue of a woman is of such a nature that but little confidence is placed in it when circumstances show that immodesty has taken possession of the heart.

Do not say, then: "The young man I love will desert me if I put a stop to these familiarities." He will do no such thing, if he be a young man worth having, but, on the contrary, he will conceive a great respect and esteem for you. Your conduct, if such as it ought to be, will cause him to be determined to secure such a prize as he esteems you to be for his own; for all true real love must be founded on respect and esteem.

But if on your rebuke, given in a decided way, though mildly at first, he leaves you, say: "Good riddance! You are no great loss." Thank God for delivering you from being bound for life to such an unsuitable companion.

Say then, when an improper familiarity is attempted: "Hands off; never dare lay a finger on me again"; "You have entirely mistaken the person," or some such thing. Show that you are offended; if the offence is more gross, leave the room, and let no doubt remain on his mind that you are deeply offended.

A wise and prudent girl may forgive such an offence once if she sees sincere regret for it, but

not when it has been repeated. If, after sufficient warning, the same conduct is repeated,
break off the acquaintance.

When such things are allowed to go on, what
is the consequence? Sin and crime; shame
and disgrace. The poor girl is deceived, and,
finally, left ruined and heart-broken, deserted
by her false lover, to bewail the consequences
of her own folly.

Another great abuse which happens sometimes is that of taking evening walks. Instead
of sitting down to talk, the affair is carried
on walking in the streets. And opportunity
enough the devil has to put forward his temptations. It is improper. Very rarely, and unless
you have confidence in the person, allow yourself to be accompanied even from one house to
another ; but avoid all wandering around for the
sake of conversation, if you would not expose
yourself to the greatest danger.

What I have said in regard to this perfect
propriety and modesty during courtship applies
to every day and every hour of it, from its beginning until the marriage takes place. Some
are so stupid as to think that as soon as they
have given their troth to another they can behave with less propriety. They say : '' We are
to be married so soon there is no need to be so
particular.'' That is not true. The obligation
to entire purity in thought, word, and deed is

as strong as ever, and God is as much offended by your violating it as if you had made no such engagement.

And when you are engaged to marry, the marriage should not be too long deferred. Long courtships are a great temptation, and give rise very often to sin which would have been avoided had they been shorter. Why put off the marriage when you have determined upon it? It is giving room to the devil to practise all his arts, either to break up the engagement or to lead you into sin. There may be reason for a certain delay; but, as a general thing, it is better to marry, notwithstanding some inconvenience, than to defer it.

Your happiness in the married state depends in a great measure on the way you conduct yourself during the courtship. You expect to receive a sacrament. You ought then to prepare for it. Holy and pure motives ought to govern you, and pure and holy conduct precede it. How can you expect God's blessing on the marriage when you have been provoking his anger by a long course of sin.

Those who do prepare well, who watch over their conduct carefully, that it may be pleasing to God in all respects, during their courtship, receive a great blessing. They have disposed themselves for grace, and in the sacrament they receive a great grace, to live happily, to love one another truly and sincerely, and to be a help to one another to secure at last the happiness of the saints in Heaven.

Bear these things in mind, and make up your minds that you will be among those who draw down an abundant grace from Heaven, rather than of the number who foolishly and thoughtlessly rush into this holy state without preparation, without prayer, and without any proper idea of its immense importance to their whole happiness for this world and for the world to come.

CHAPTER LXXXI.

THE RIGHT IDEA OF MARRIED LIFE.

MANY have an overstrained and false view of matrimony, which leads to great unhappiness afterwards. They are of a fanciful disposition, fond of building castles in the air, and overlooking the realities of life.

Besides, they have heard many highly-wrought stories and legends of princes and princesses, of lords and ladies, of village girls and their admirers, who were dying of love to one another. The lovers are, of course, perfection itself. The young man is tall and handsome; the young woman fair and beautiful. He is noble and generous; she has every amiable quality of woman. In short, two such mortals could not be found anywhere else in the whole world.

They go through all sorts of trials for one another. He is ready to die a dozen times for her sake, and she is ready to make away with herself quite as often when the course of true love does not run smooth. After a wonderful series of ups and downs, and astonishing surprises, all comes out right; they get married, and that is the last we hear of them.

This is the stuff we get in novels and romances, and it has turned many a poor girl's head and ruined her happiness. Novels represent marriage as the end of our existence. It is not so. God is the object and end of our existence. Novels represent a husband as in the place of God to us. It is not so. The love of a husband cannot fill the heart. It is only God's love that can do that.

If you place your supreme good and happiness in the love of your husband, you will be sure to be disappointed. Trouble and anxiety will be mixed with it, and death will be likely to knock your idol to pieces.

If you imagine you are going to live like two angels together, seeing only perfection in one another, and admiring all you see, I rather think you will be mistaken. Lovers are blind; they hide their faults and show only their amiable qualities; they are not willing to see faults when they are only too plain, but by and by there will be plenty of time to find out the truth and no motive for concealment.

He comes to see you in his Sunday's best, his shoes shining and his hair brushed and oiled; by and by his face will look dirty and coarse, his hair all disorder, his clothes begrimed with dirt.

He talks soft and delicate now; by and by you will hear harsh sounds out of his mouth. "Why haven't you done this?" "Why don't you do better?" and perhaps things a great deal worse.

He was ready to die for you awhile ago, but you find he lives a great deal more for himself than for you. You find him cross and disagreeable, lazy, perhaps, and shiftless, selfish and dissipated, provoking and inconsiderate; in short, you discover many things which you did not dream of before.

And I dare say you will show many traits of character which he did not see before, and which will require a good deal of forbearance to put up with.

People who form great expectations are apt to get disappointed; and the higher one's hopes the more cruel the disappointment. Young people whose ideas of marriage are of the fanciful kind, gotten out of novels, who imagine that married life is a perpetual courtship or honey-moon, that love is going to prevent all that is disagreeable, that love will supply bread and butter, keep the children from crying, or the weather pleasant, or get the dinner, or make the beds, will sometimes find themselves cruelly un-deceived.

Their ideas are false and they cannot be real-ized. Now comes the danger. They give way to the disappointment. They begin to hate where they thought they loved. Bickering and dissension set in. After awhile they live pretty much like cats and dogs, and there is no reme-dy but a separation—a miserable remedy, which is directly in the face of the solemn promise they made to God to take each other for better or worse.

If they had looked at the matter in its true light, there would have been no disappointment. Their chief happiness would not have been placed in one another, but higher, in God our only True Good. They would have had some-thing to fall back upon in case of disappoint-ment.

They would have expected many and great faults of character in one another, to be borne patiently and put up with, and have been pre-pared for the worst.

When a couple love one another in God and for God—which is the only real true love worth having—God's grace is sufficient for them. All looks different. They learn to respect one another, to make each other happy, and increase in love every day.

Look at marriage, then, in this light. Put away fancy and look at the reality, and pray God to give you His true light, to see things as they are, and for grace to act accordingly.

CHAPTER LXXXII.

OF THE MARRIAGE CEREMONY.

WHEN all has been settled, and the day appointed, take care that all shall be arranged in a manner suitable to the importance and holiness of the sacrament which you then receive.

Marriage is not merely a state of life instituted by God, but a sacrament. The union of man and woman represents the union of Christ and his church, and therefore it is a sacred thing.

You should regard it in that light, and prepare for it with as much care as you would prepare for your communion. There are special reasons for not neglecting this. The happiness and well-being of your life, and very likely of your eternity, depend upon it. You need special grace, and all you can obtain, to sanctify it.   Think of these things a good while beforehand, and pray frequently and fervently.

Look at the matter in a spiritual point of view, and purify your intention, looking only to the will of God, and how you may be able to serve Him better.

We have a beautiful example of this in Scripture, in the case of Tobias and Sara.   They spent three days in devout prayer that God might sanctify their marriage.   " For we are the children of the saints," said they, " and we must not be joined together like the heathens that know not God " (Tobias viii. 5).

Have the laws of the church in regard to the publication of the banns observed.   These laws are wise and good, intended to prevent persons who have no right to marry one another from attempting it.   Many an unfortunate girl has been deceived into an unlawful marriage because the banns were not published.

If there is no danger whatever of such a thing happening to you, never mind, get your banns published.   Uphold God's laws and set a good example to others.   Do not ask a dispensation unless you have a solid reason for it.   It is no good reason because you do not like to be published.

Why should you go about your marriage in a stealthy and secret manner?   You are not going to steal any one's property ; you are not going to do anything mean or dishonorable ; on the contrary, you enter an honorable state, one worthy of respect among all men ; as Scripture says : "Marriage is honorable in all" (Heb. xiii. 4).

Let all things about the wedding be proper and suitable. Avoid idle display and useless extravagance in regard to dress. See that all is proper about the entertainment, if there is one. In short, draw down God's blessing on the marriage by your care that there shall be nothing to offend Him in the way you enter upon it. So may you hope to continue it in happiness and make it a great means for your eternal salvation.

CHAPTER LXXXIII.

HOW TO BEHAVE IN SICKNESS.—CONCLUSION.

BEFORE closing this book I wish to say a few words on how a good girl should look upon sickness, and behave herself in it.

Sickness, like everything else which God allows to befall us, is intended for our good. If we take it in the right spirit it will prove an immense advantage to us.

Sickness affords us an opportunity to practise

many virtues in a high degree, particularly those most excellent ones of humility and patience. When stretched upon the bed of sickness, we feel how helpless we are of ourselves, and how completely we depend on God for health and strength and every breath we draw. We cry to him and He hears us, and helps us. Sickness is a time of grace.

What an opportunity it gives us for patience, amid so many pains and privations and wants.

If we did but know, it is just the time to be like our Lord Jesus Christ as He was hanging, so racked with torment and so afflicted, upon His cross for our redemption.

Particularly is this the case with a poor girl who lives out, when she is taken down by sickness. Among strangers, with no kind mother at hand to take tender care of her, how forsaken she must feel herself at such a time !

She is working for hire, and when she gets sick her employers very likely think far more of their own loss of her services than of her condition. She lacks that attention and kindness that they would pay one of their own family. She cannot expect those delicacies and that constant nursing that near relatives would be likely to give her.

Indeed, in most cases, she will be obliged to be removed elsewhere, and to provide for herself as best she can, for it cannot be expected, or required, that her employers take care of her.

They have agreed to pay her wages in return for service, and, of course, when she cannot afford that service she becomes a burden upon them, and in justice has no more claim to be taken care of than any other person. Besides, in many cases it is quite out of the power of her employers to take so great a burden upon themselves.

On all these accounts sickness is, to the girl who lives out, a great trial and a great opportunity to practise heroic virtue.

Let her then, in such case, place all her hope and all her confidence in God, in our Lord Jesus Christ. Let her accept all as coming from His hands, for it is the truth His blessed hands have held out this cup for her to drink, as a most salutary and good medicine for her soul.

Let her not be satisfied with accepting it, but keep thanking Him for it, and saying to herself that it is the very best thing for her, and that she would not have it otherwise than as God wills.

Now is the time for patience, to keep down all murmuring and dissatisfaction. No doubt there will be temptation to murmur, but put it all aside, for God is as good now as ever, and it is wrong now as ever to complain of what you cannot help and He has allowed.

If the family where you are cannot help you,
go willingly elsewhere. Do not indulge in useless hard feeling. Consider all right, and look
only at the Divine will.

If they care for you, be very grateful and
thankful for what you had no right to expect.
Do not, in any case, be fretful and impatient
after any want of attention, or if anything you
need or desire is wanting. Remember how our
Lord needed a little water to moisten His tongue
as He was hanging upon the cross.

Some girls, when they get sick, particularly
if they are not used to it, show a deal of impatience ; they give a great deal of unnecessary
trouble, and show an unthankful spirit in regard
to what is done for them. This is certainly
quite the wrong spirit, and one that renders
such a girl very unhappy herself and displeasing
to God.

But, on the contrary, I must say the examples of holy patience and peace under affliction,
on the part of others, is oftentimes most beautiful ; all who witness it are charmed and edified
by it. What stores of merit such a girl lays up
for herself and for others !

She really preaches the Gospel of our Lord
Jesus Christ, and does much to save souls ; for
her example is more effectual than perhaps the
words of the most eloquent preacher can be.

You cannot do much in sickness in the way

of set prayers and devotions, but you can do a great deal in the way of patience and resignation. You can do a great deal in the way of short, fervent ejaculations, such as, "Thy holy will be done"; "Grant me patience"; "Praise God for His goodness"; or many others of the same sort.

You can offer yourself to God entirely, giving up your life, if it be God's will, cheerfully into His hands. For the rest, keep as quiet and cheerful as possible, putting away all temptations and troubles of whatever sort they may be, and trusting entirely to God and our Lord Jesus Christ, just as an infant reposes with confidence in the arms of its mother.

So, if it be God's will, this blessed time of sickness will land you safe on the shore of eternity, to enjoy for ever, and with joy unspeakable, the sight of God, the society of Jesus Christ, of the Blessed Virgin Mary, and of all holy saints who have "fought the good fight of faith" and received the immortal crown of victory.

And now I must bring my work to a close. I have done my best to teach you those principles of religion and virtue which will insure you a happy and joyful life here, and the rewards of eternity.

It has cost me much labor and reflection, but I have been glad to give it, because I know it will be appreciated by grateful hearts. May God smile upon it! May the Blessed Virgin Mary and the Saints take it under their protection!

And if any good girl shall find herself benefited by reading this book, and the love of God increased in her heart, I beg she will not forget the author in her prayers, but beg of God for me that I may lead a good life here, with a single eye to His glory, and attain everlasting life hereafter.

God bless you all!

THE END.